# ZERO POINT
# WEIGHT LOSS COOKBOOK

**Nataly Summers**

**Disclaimer and legal note**.

The information contained in this book and its contents are not intended to replace any form of medical or professional advice; nor is it meant to substitute the need for medical, financial, legal, or other advice or services that may be required. The content and information in this book are provided for educational and recreational purposes only.

The content and information contained in this book have been compiled from sources considered reliable and are accurate according to the knowledge, information, and beliefs of the Author. However, the Author cannot guarantee their accuracy and validity and therefore cannot be held responsible for any errors and/or omissions. Furthermore, changes are periodically made to this book as necessary. When appropriate and/or necessary, you should consult a professional (including, but not limited to, your doctor, lawyer, financial advisor, or other such professionals) before using any remedy, technique, and/or information suggested in this book.

By using the contents and information in this book, you agree to hold the Author free from any harm, cost, and expense, including legal fees that may result from the application of any of the information contained in this book. This disclaimer applies to any loss, damage, or injury caused by the application of the contents of this book, directly or indirectly, in violation of a contract, tort, negligence, personal injury, criminal intent, or under any other circumstance.

You agree to accept all risks arising from the use of the information presented in this book.

You agree that, by continuing to read this book, when appropriate and/or necessary, you will consult a professional (including, but not limited to, your doctor, lawyer, financial advisor, or other such professionals) before using the remedies, techniques, or information suggested in this book.

# TABLE OF CONTENT

# INTRODUCTION

## *OVERVIEW OF THE DIET*

In the intricate tapestry of contemporary dietary regimes, where each new trend competes for supremacy with the promise of effortless transformation, the "0 Point Diet Cookbook for Beginners" emerges as a beacon of clarity and practicality. This tome, meticulously crafted for novices and those disenchanted with the perennial cycle of dieting disappointment, offers a refreshingly straightforward approach rooted in the proven principles of the Weight Watchers program.

The cornerstone of the Diet is the concept of Zero Point foods—those nutritional treasures that can be consumed without the burden of meticulous tracking or the constant fear of overindulgence. This innovative system is designed to liberate rather than constrain, to simplify rather than complicate. By focusing on a diverse array of foods that are both nourishing and satisfying, the 0 Point Diet facilitates a harmonious relationship with eating, fostering a lifestyle that is both sustainable and enjoyable.

At its essence, the Diet champions the consumption of foods that are rich in nutrients yet low in calories. These include an abundance of fresh fruits, vibrant vegetables, lean proteins, legumes, and non-fat dairy products. These foods are meticulously selected to ensure they contribute significantly to one's nutritional needs while minimizing the risk of weight gain. This approach contrasts sharply with many traditional diets that impose severe restrictions and foster an adversarial relationship with food.

Why does the 0 Point Diet resonate so deeply with its adherents? The answer lies in its elegant simplicity and its respect for the individual's autonomy. Unlike diets that require rigid adherence to complex rules and exhaustive calorie counting, the Diet empowers individuals to make wholesome choices without the constant oversight of a dietary ledger. This freedom allows for a more intuitive and less stressful eating experience, which is crucial for long-term adherence and success.

However, it is essential to understand that it is not an invitation to abandon all dietary discretion. While it encourages generous consumption of Zero Point foods, it also implicitly advises moderation with foods that are higher in calories and lower in nutritional value, such as processed snacks, sugary beverages, and high-fat dairy products. By striking this balance, the diet ensures that followers receive comprehensive nutrition without unnecessary caloric excess.

For the uninitiated, the prospect of adopting a new dietary regimen can be daunting. Yet, the "0 Point Diet Cookbook for Beginners" is meticulously designed to guide readers through this transition with ease and confidence. It provides not only an extensive selection of recipes but also practical advice on meal planning, grocery shopping, and cooking techniques. This holistic approach ensures that even those with minimal culinary experience can embark on their dietary journey with assurance.

The 0 Point Diet is more than a mere strategy for weight loss; it is a philosophy that promotes overall well-being. It emphasizes the joy of eating a variety of wholesome foods without the constant anxiety of dietary restrictions. By fostering a positive relationship with food, the diet helps individuals to not only achieve their weight loss goals but also to enjoy a more balanced and fulfilling lifestyle.

## *The Benefits of Zero Point Foods*

In the ever-evolving landscape of dietary advice, where complexity often reigns supreme, the 0 Point Diet stands out for its simplicity and practicality. Central to this approach is the concept of Zero Point foods—nutrient-dense, low-calorie options that can be consumed without the meticulous counting and tracking often associated with traditional diets. This foundational pillar of the Diet offers a myriad of benefits, each contributing to a healthier, more sustainable way of eating.

1. **Promotes Satiety and Reduces Hunger Pangs**
Zero Point foods are generally high in fiber, protein, and water content, which help to keep you feeling fuller for longer periods. This satiety reduces the temptation to snack on less healthy options between meals, making it easier to adhere to your dietary goals without feeling deprived. For instance, fruits and vegetables like apples, berries, cucumbers, and spinach are not only refreshing but also filling.

2. **Encourages Nutrient-Rich Eating**
By emphasizing foods that are inherently low in calories but rich in essential vitamins, minerals, and antioxidants, the 0 Point Diet ensures that your nutritional needs are met without excessive calorie intake. This focus on nutrient density supports overall health, boosts immune function, and can help prevent chronic diseases. Lean proteins, such as chicken breast, turkey breast, and most fish, provide essential amino acids crucial for muscle maintenance and repair.

3. **Simplifies Meal Planning and Preparation**
One of the significant advantages of Zero Point foods is the ease they bring to meal planning and preparation. Without the need to weigh, measure, or track these foods meticulously, you can focus on enjoying the cooking process and experimenting with new recipes. This simplicity encourages more home-cooked meals, which are typically healthier than takeout or processed foods. For busy individuals, this can be a game-changer, making it feasible to maintain a healthy diet even with a hectic schedule.

4. **Reduces Dietary Stress and Anxiety**
The psychological freedom provided by this Diet cannot be overstated. By removing the constant pressure to count every calorie and track every bite, this approach reduces dietary stress and anxiety. This mental ease translates into a more relaxed and positive relationship with food, which is essential for long-term adherence to any dietary plan. The diet fosters a sense of autonomy, allowing individuals to eat intuitively while still achieving their health and weight loss goals.

5. **Supports Sustainable Weight Loss**
Zero Point foods facilitate weight loss by creating a natural calorie deficit without the feeling of restriction. As these foods can be eaten freely, they enable you to manage hunger effectively, which is a critical factor in sustainable weight loss. By prioritizing foods that are naturally low in calories and high in volume, the diet helps to reduce overall calorie intake while still allowing for satisfying, substantial meals.

6. **Versatile and Adaptable to Various Lifestyles**
Whether you are a vegetarian, pescatarian, or an omnivore, the 0 Point Diet is versatile enough to accommodate a wide range of dietary preferences and lifestyles. This flexibility makes it accessible to a broad audience, ensuring that everyone can find Zero Point foods that they enjoy and that fit their unique dietary needs. The inclusion of legumes, non-fat dairy products, and a variety of fruits and vegetables ensures there is something for everyone.

7. **Encourages Healthy Eating Habits**
By focusing on wholesome, unprocessed foods, the 0 Point Diet naturally encourages healthier eating habits. This shift away from processed snacks, sugary beverages, and high-fat foods not only aids in

weight loss but also improves overall health outcomes. Over time, these healthier habits become ingrained, leading to a more balanced and nutritious diet long after the initial weight loss goals have been achieved.

# CHAPTER 1
# GETTING STARTED

## *1.1 DEFINING ZERO POINT FOODS*

In the labyrinth of modern dietary plans, where complexity often overshadows clarity, the concept of foods that do not count against one's daily intake allowance emerges as a beacon of simplicity and efficacy. These foods are the backbone of this approach, carefully chosen for their ability to nourish the body without adding unnecessary calories. But what exactly qualifies a food for this esteemed category? The answer lies in a meticulous evaluation of its nutritional profile, caloric content, and overall impact on satiety and metabolic health.

Zero Point foods are, in essence, those that you can consume in abundance without the need to track their intake meticulously. They are primarily nutrient-dense, low-calorie foods that provide significant health benefits while being naturally low in fats and sugars. This categorization includes an array of fresh fruits and vegetables, lean proteins, certain dairy products, and legumes. The rationale behind their selection is grounded in their ability to fill you up, not out, promoting a sense of fullness and satisfaction that can help curb overeating and support weight management.

Fruits and vegetables are at the heart of this concept. These foods are celebrated for their high fiber content, vitamins, and minerals. For instance, apples, berries, and oranges are not only delicious but also rich in antioxidants and fiber, contributing to digestive health and reducing the risk of chronic diseases. Vegetables such as leafy greens, cucumbers, and bell peppers are low in calories yet packed with essential nutrients like vitamins A and C, potassium, and folate. These characteristics make them ideal for creating meals that are both nutritious and satisfying.

Lean proteins also play a crucial role. Skinless chicken breast, turkey, most fish, and shellfish provide the necessary amino acids for muscle maintenance and repair without the added fats that can contribute to weight gain. Eggs and tofu are also included, offering versatile options for various culinary preferences and dietary restrictions. These proteins help keep you full for longer periods, reducing the temptation to snack between meals.

Non-fat dairy products, such as plain Greek yogurt and cottage cheese, are included due to their calcium and protein content. These items support bone health and provide a creamy texture that can enhance a variety of dishes, from smoothies to savory sauces. Their low-fat content ensures that they contribute minimally to the daily calorie count while providing essential nutrients.

Legumes, including beans, lentils, and chickpeas, are another staple. These foods are high in protein and fiber, making them a valuable addition to any meal. They are particularly beneficial for vegetarians and those looking to reduce meat consumption, offering a plant-based protein source that is both filling and nutritious.

The philosophy behind these foods is not just about what you eat, but how you eat. It encourages a mindful approach to eating, focusing on the quality of the food rather than the quantity. By emphasizing foods that are naturally filling and nutritionally dense, this approach helps individuals build a positive relationship with food, where the goal is to nourish the body and enjoy the eating experience, rather than merely counting calories or restricting intake.

## 1.2 NUTRITIONAL BENEFITS

The inclusion of Zero Point foods in one's diet offers an array of nutritional benefits that extend far beyond the scope of weight management. These foods are chosen not merely for their low-calorie content but for their rich nutrient profiles that contribute to overall health and well-being. By incorporating a diverse selection of these foods into your daily meals, you are not only supporting your weight loss goals but also enhancing your body's ability to function optimally.

One of the most significant benefits of these foods is their high fiber content. Dietary fiber, found abundantly in fruits, vegetables, and legumes, plays a crucial role in digestive health. It helps maintain regular bowel movements, prevents constipation, and supports a healthy gut microbiome. The presence of fiber in the diet also contributes to prolonged satiety, reducing hunger pangs and helping to control overall food intake. This is particularly beneficial for those who struggle with snacking between meals or late-night cravings.

In addition to fiber, these foods are packed with essential vitamins and minerals. Fruits such as berries, oranges, and apples are rich in vitamin C, which is vital for immune function and skin health. Leafy greens like spinach and kale provide vitamins A and K, essential for vision and bone health, respectively. The diverse range of vitamins and minerals found in these foods ensures that your body receives the necessary nutrients to support various physiological functions, from energy production to cellular repair.

Lean proteins included in this category offer numerous health benefits. Proteins are the building blocks of the body, necessary for muscle maintenance, repair, and growth. Skinless chicken breast, turkey, fish, and shellfish are excellent sources of high-quality protein that are low in saturated fats. These proteins not only help in building and maintaining muscle mass but also play a crucial role in metabolic health, supporting enzyme function and hormone production.

Non-fat dairy products provide a good source of calcium and probiotics. Calcium is essential for maintaining strong bones and teeth, while probiotics found in yogurt support digestive health by promoting a healthy balance of gut bacteria. These dairy products offer a creamy texture that can enhance various dishes without adding excessive calories or fat.

Legumes, another cornerstone of this dietary approach, are rich in plant-based protein and iron. Iron is crucial for the production of hemoglobin, which transports oxygen in the blood. Consuming legumes helps in preventing iron deficiency anemia and boosts overall energy levels. The high fiber content in legumes also supports heart health by helping to lower cholesterol levels.

Another notable benefit is the presence of antioxidants in these foods. Antioxidants, such as those found in berries, tomatoes, and leafy greens, help combat oxidative stress in the body. Oxidative stress can lead to cellular damage and contribute to the development of chronic diseases, including cancer and heart disease. By neutralizing free radicals, antioxidants support overall health and longevity, promoting a healthier aging process.

## 1.3 Common Zero Point Foods List

To fully embrace this dietary approach, it is essential to familiarize yourself with the foods that you can enjoy freely. These foods, carefully selected for their nutritional value and low-calorie content, form the foundation of your meals, ensuring that you can eat to satisfaction without compromising your health goals. Here is a comprehensive list of the most common foods that fall into this category, organized by food groups for your convenience.

Fruits are a delightful and nutritious component, offering natural sweetness and a wealth of vitamins and fiber. Most fresh, frozen, or canned fruits (without added sugar) are included. This category encompasses apples, apricots, bananas, blackberries, blueberries, cantaloupe, cherries, grapefruit, grapes, kiwis, lemons and limes, mangoes, oranges, peaches, pears, pineapples, plums, raspberries, strawberries, and watermelon. These fruits provide a variety of nutrients, including vitamin C, potassium, and dietary fiber, contributing to overall health and satiety.

Non-starchy vegetables are celebrated for their low-calorie content and high nutritional value. The list of such vegetables includes artichokes, arugula, asparagus, beets, bell peppers, broccoli, Brussels sprouts, cabbage, carrots, cauliflower, celery, cucumbers, eggplant, garlic, green beans, kale, lettuce, mushrooms, onions, peppers (all types), radishes, spinach, squash (summer and zucchini), tomatoes, turnips, watercress, and zucchini. These vegetables are rich in vitamins A, C, and K, as well as minerals like potassium and magnesium, and are essential for maintaining a balanced diet.

Lean proteins are pivotal in supporting muscle maintenance and satiety. Included are skinless chicken breast, skinless turkey breast, most fish (including tuna, salmon, cod, and tilapia), shellfish (such as shrimp, crab, and lobster), eggs, and tofu (firm or soft). These proteins are high in essential amino acids and low in saturated fats, making them ideal for a health-conscious diet.

Legumes are a rich source of plant-based protein and fiber, aiding in digestive health and providing sustained energy. The list includes black beans, chickpeas, kidney beans, lentils, navy beans, and pinto beans. These legumes are versatile ingredients that can be used in soups, stews, salads, and more, contributing to a diverse and satisfying diet.

Non-fat dairy products provide calcium and probiotics, essential for bone health and digestion. Included are plain non-fat Greek yogurt and plain non-fat cottage cheese. Incorporating these dairy options into daily meals can help ensure adequate calcium intake without added fats or sugars.

Non-caloric broths are a flavorful base for soups and stews, enhancing the taste of dishes without contributing to the point count. Included are vegetable broth, chicken broth (non-fat), and beef broth (non-fat). These broths add depth to recipes while keeping them within dietary guidelines.

While not necessarily categorized as foods, herbs and spices play a crucial role in making dishes flavorful and enjoyable. Fresh and dried herbs, along with spices, are inherently zero points and can be used liberally to enhance the taste of meals.

This comprehensive list underscores the versatility and nutritional richness of these foods. By incorporating

them into daily meals, individuals can enjoy a diverse, satisfying, and health-promoting diet without the need for meticulous tracking. This approach not only aids in weight management but also ensures that individuals receive the necessary nutrients to maintain overall health and well-being.

# CHAPTER 2

# ESSENTIAL TOOLS AND TIPS

## 2.1 *Must-Have Kitchen Tools*

In the pursuit of culinary excellence, having the right tools at your disposal is paramount. The foundation of any well-equipped kitchen begins with a selection of essential tools designed to streamline the cooking process and enhance the overall experience. Whether you are a seasoned chef or a novice cook, these tools are indispensable in crafting nutritious and delicious meals efficiently and effectively.

A high-quality **chef's knife** is arguably the most important tool in the kitchen. Its versatility allows it to handle a multitude of tasks, from chopping vegetables to slicing meats with precision. A sharp, well-balanced chef's knife reduces the effort required to prepare ingredients and increases safety by minimizing the risk of slips and cuts. Investing in a durable, ergonomic knife ensures that meal preparation is both efficient and enjoyable.

Equally important is a sturdy **cutting board**. Opt for a board that is both durable and easy to clean. Wooden cutting boards are often preferred for their durability and gentle impact on knife blades, while plastic boards are praised for their ease of sanitation. A spacious cutting board provides ample room for chopping and slicing, facilitating a smoother workflow and reducing clutter on your countertops.

A **non-stick skillet** is another cornerstone of the well-equipped kitchen. The non-stick surface allows for cooking with minimal or no oil, which aligns perfectly with healthy eating principles. This skillet is ideal for sautéing vegetables, preparing lean proteins, and cooking eggs without sticking. A high-quality non-stick skillet ensures easy food release and simplifies cleaning, making it a practical choice for everyday use.

For those who enjoy a variety of textures in their meals, a **steamer basket** is an excellent addition. Steaming is a gentle cooking method that preserves the nutritional integrity and vibrant colors of vegetables. A steamer basket fits into most pots and can be used to cook a wide range of vegetables, from broccoli and carrots to leafy greens. This tool is essential for maintaining the nutritional quality of your meals while adding variety to your cooking methods.

A **food processor** is another versatile tool that can significantly enhance your culinary repertoire. It can chop, slice, dice, and puree with speed and consistency, making it invaluable for preparing ingredients quickly and efficiently. This tool is particularly useful for creating homemade dips, sauces, and dressings, such as hummus or tomato salsa, which can complement a wide range of dishes. The food processor's ability to handle multiple tasks reduces preparation time and encourages the use of fresh, whole ingredients.

A set of **mixing bowls** in various sizes is essential for any kitchen. These bowls are used for mixing ingredients, serving salads, and storing prepped food. Stainless steel mixing bowls are particularly durable and easy to clean, making them a practical choice for everyday use. Their versatility ensures they can be used in a multitude of ways, enhancing the efficiency of meal preparation.

A **digital kitchen scale** is invaluable for those who are serious about precision in their cooking. While the focus of this dietary approach is on the quality of foods rather than quantity, there are times when accurate measurement is necessary, especially when following new recipes or ensuring portion control. A digital scale provides precise measurements, ensuring consistency in cooking and baking, which is crucial for achieving the desired results.

Measuring cups and spoons are also fundamental tools in the kitchen. These tools ensure that ingredients are measured accurately, which is particularly important when baking or following complex recipes. Using the correct measurements helps to maintain the balance of flavors and textures in your dishes.

Lastly, having a variety of **storage containers** is essential for keeping your kitchen organized and your food fresh. Airtight containers of various sizes are ideal for storing prepped ingredients, leftovers, and bulk pantry items. They help to maintain the freshness of your food and make it easy to see what you have on hand, reducing waste and ensuring that you always have the necessary ingredients at your fingertips.

## 2.2 Stocking Your Pantry

A well-stocked pantry is the cornerstone of a successful kitchen, providing the foundation for countless meals and ensuring that you always have the essentials on hand. Properly stocking your pantry involves more than just having the basics; it requires thoughtful selection and organization of ingredients that align with your dietary goals and culinary preferences. Here, we delve into the essentials of a well-stocked pantry and offer tips for maintaining an organized and efficient food supply.

To begin with, **grains and legumes** are fundamental components of any pantry. Whole grains such as quinoa, brown rice, and oats are versatile and nutritious, serving as the base for many dishes. They are high in fiber and essential nutrients, making them a valuable addition to your diet. Legumes, including black beans, lentils, and chickpeas, provide plant-based protein and can be used in a variety of recipes, from soups and stews to salads and sides. Stocking these items in bulk ensures that you always have a hearty, nutritious option at your disposal.

**Canned goods** are another pantry staple that can significantly enhance meal preparation. Look for canned tomatoes, tomato paste, and a variety of beans. These items are convenient, shelf-stable, and can be used to create a myriad of dishes. When selecting canned goods, opt for low-sodium or no-salt-added versions to maintain control over the sodium content of your meals. Canned fruits in their own juice (not syrup) are also a great addition, providing a convenient and healthy snack option.

A selection of **vinegars and oils** is essential for adding flavor and depth to your dishes. Apple cider vinegar, balsamic vinegar, and red wine vinegar are versatile and can be used in marinades, dressings, and as finishing touches. While oils like olive oil and avocado oil are not zero points, they are healthy fats that should be used sparingly. A spray bottle can help control portions, ensuring you benefit from their flavor and health properties without exceeding your dietary limits.

**Herbs and spices** are crucial for making meals flavorful and enjoyable. Stock your pantry with a variety of dried herbs and spices, such as garlic powder, onion powder, cumin, paprika, oregano, basil, thyme, and rosemary. These ingredients add depth and complexity to your dishes without adding extra calories. Fresh herbs can also be dried and stored, providing an aromatic addition to your cooking. Spices not only enhance the flavor of your meals but also offer various health benefits, from anti-inflammatory properties to aiding digestion.

**Nuts and seeds** are another valuable addition to your pantry. Almonds, walnuts, chia seeds, and flaxseeds provide healthy fats, protein, and fiber. They can be used in a variety of ways, from adding crunch to salads and yogurt to serving as a nutritious snack. Store these items in airtight containers to maintain their freshness and extend their shelf life.

**Broths and stocks** are indispensable for adding richness and flavor to soups, stews, and sauces. Vegetable, chicken, and beef broths are versatile and can be used in a wide range of recipes. Opt for low-sodium or no-salt-added versions to keep your dishes heart-healthy and within dietary guidelines. These broths add depth to your recipes while keeping them within the principles of healthy eating.

**Non-fat dairy products** should also be part of your pantry staples. Plain non-fat Greek yogurt and non-fat cottage cheese are versatile ingredients that can be used in both savory and sweet dishes. These items provide a good source of calcium and protein without the extra calories and fat found in their full-fat counterparts. Their versatility makes them indispensable in creating satisfying, healthy meals.

**Frozen fruits and vegetables** are an excellent addition to your pantry, providing convenient options that retain their nutritional value. Stock your freezer with a variety of frozen fruits, such as berries and mangoes, and vegetables, such as spinach, broccoli, and peas. These items can be easily incorporated into smoothies, soups, and stir-fries, ensuring that you always have nutritious options on hand.

## *2.3 Organizational Tips for Efficiency*

Efficiency in the kitchen is about more than just speed; it is about creating an environment where everything you need is within reach and easy to find. A well-organized kitchen not only makes meal preparation more efficient but also more enjoyable. Here, we offer practical organizational tips designed to enhance your kitchen's functionality and streamline your cooking process.

The first step to achieving an organized kitchen is **decluttering**. A cluttered kitchen can impede your ability to cook efficiently and enjoyably. Start by evaluating your kitchen tools and appliances, keeping only those you regularly use. Items that serve little purpose should be stored away or donated. This initial step creates a clean slate, making it easier to organize your space effectively.

**Optimizing your kitchen layout** is crucial for efficiency. The concept of the kitchen work triangle, comprising the sink, stove, and refrigerator, is fundamental to efficient kitchen design. Ensure these three points are easily accessible, with minimal obstacles in between. This layout minimizes unnecessary movement, allowing you to move fluidly between tasks. Consider the placement of your most-used items within this triangle to further enhance your workflow.

A well-organized **pantry** is the heart of an efficient kitchen. Group similar items together, such as spices, grains, and canned goods, and use clear, labeled containers to store them. This not only keeps your pantry tidy but also makes it easy to see when you're running low on essentials.

Consider using tiered shelves or risers to maximize vertical space, ensuring all items are visible and accessible.

For frequently used items, create a dedicated **cooking station**. This can include a section of your countertop where you keep your most-used tools, such as knives, cutting boards, and mixing bowls. Having these items readily available reduces the time spent searching for them, making meal prep more efficient. Additionally, keep a utensil holder next to the stove with your most-used cooking tools, such as spatulas, tongs, and wooden spoons.

Incorporating a **labeling system** can further enhance efficiency. Label shelves, drawers, and containers to ensure everything has a designated place. This not only helps you locate items quickly but also makes it easier to maintain an organized space. For pantry items, consider labeling with both the contents and the date of purchase to keep track of freshness and avoid waste.

**Meal planning** is another critical component of kitchen efficiency. Dedicate a specific time each week to plan your meals, create a shopping list, and prep ingredients. This foresight can significantly reduce the stress of daily meal preparation and ensure you always have the necessary ingredients on hand. Use a whiteboard or a planner to keep track of your meal plans and grocery lists, making it easy to reference throughout the week.

To further streamline meal prep, consider **batch cooking**. Prepare larger quantities of staples such as grains, legumes, and proteins, and store them in the refrigerator or freezer for quick assembly throughout the week. This approach not only saves time but also ensures you have healthy options readily available, reducing the temptation to reach for less nutritious alternatives.

Efficient **storage solutions** are also vital. Use stackable containers to maximize fridge and pantry space, and invest in high-quality storage bags or vacuum sealers to keep ingredients fresh for longer. Drawer dividers and shelf organizers can help keep smaller items in order, ensuring that everything has its place and is easy to find.

Maintaining a **clean workspace** is crucial for efficiency. Develop the habit of cleaning as you go, washing dishes, and wiping down surfaces as you cook. This practice not only keeps your kitchen tidy but also reduces the amount of cleanup needed after meals, making the entire cooking process more enjoyable.

# CHAPTER 3
# SMART SHOPPING

## 3.1 *How to Shop Smart for Zero Point Foods*

Mastering the art of shopping smartly is crucial for anyone looking to maintain a nutritious and balanced diet. Smart shopping ensures that your kitchen is always stocked with essential ingredients, enabling you to create wholesome meals effortlessly. Here are some key strategies to help you shop efficiently and effectively.

Preparation is the foundation of smart shopping. Begin by planning your meals for the week. This not only helps in creating a focused shopping list but also minimizes the chances of impulse buys that often lead to unhealthy choices. By breaking down your meal plans into necessary ingredients, you can ensure that your list includes a variety of fruits, vegetables, lean proteins, legumes, and non-fat dairy products. This approach not only saves time but also ensures that you have everything you need to prepare nutritious meals throughout the week.

When crafting your shopping list, categorize items by their location in the store. Grouping produce, dairy, and pantry staples together can streamline your shopping trip, making it more efficient and reducing the time spent wandering the aisles. This organized approach helps you stick to your list and avoid unnecessary purchases.

The produce section should be your primary focus. Fresh fruits and vegetables are the backbone of a nutritious diet, providing essential nutrients, fiber, and flavor. Prioritize a colorful array of produce to ensure a diverse intake of vitamins and minerals. Seasonal fruits and vegetables not only offer peak flavor but are often more affordable and environmentally friendly. Look for items such as leafy greens, berries, apples, bell peppers, cucumbers, and tomatoes. These items can be used in a variety of dishes, from salads to stews, ensuring that your meals are both nutritious and exciting.

Lean proteins are another critical component of a balanced diet. When shopping for proteins, opt for skinless chicken breast, turkey breast, fish, and shellfish. These items are low in fat and high in essential amino acids, supporting muscle maintenance and overall health. For those who prefer plant-based options, tofu and legumes such as black beans, lentils, and chickpeas are excellent choices. Ensure that any canned legumes are low-sodium or no-salt-added to align with dietary guidelines.

The dairy aisle can be a bit tricky, but it's essential to focus on non-fat options. Plain non-fat Greek yogurt and non-fat cottage cheese are versatile ingredients that can be used in both savory and sweet dishes. These items provide a good source of calcium and protein without the added calories and fat found in their full-fat counterparts.

When navigating the aisles for pantry staples, choose whole grains like quinoa and brown rice, which, although not zero points, are beneficial when consumed in moderation. Additionally, stock up on vinegars such as apple cider and balsamic, which can enhance the flavor of your dishes without adding points. Herbs and spices are also vital, providing a way to add depth and variety to your meals. Keep a well-stocked spice rack with items like garlic powder, cumin, paprika, and basil.

Be mindful of the labels when purchasing packaged goods. Look for items with minimal ingredients and avoid those with added sugars, unhealthy fats, and high sodium content. Products labeled as "low-fat" or "diet" are not always the healthiest options as they may contain added sugars or artificial ingredients to compensate for the reduced fat content.

Bulk buying can be both economical and practical, especially for non-perishable items like dried legumes, grains, and spices. However, it's important to store these items properly to maintain their freshness. Invest in airtight containers and label them with the purchase date to ensure you use the oldest items first.

In conclusion, smart shopping for Zero Point foods is an integral part of maintaining a healthy and balanced diet. By preparing ahead, making informed choices, and being mindful of labels, you can stock your kitchen with ingredients that not only align with your dietary goals but also inspire delicious, healthy meals. This strategic approach to shopping ensures that you are always equipped to create zero-point dishes, making the path to a healthier lifestyle both accessible and sustainable.

## *3.2 Budget-Friendly Shopping Tips*

Maintaining a healthy diet doesn't have to break the bank. With some strategic planning and smart shopping techniques, you can keep your grocery bill in check while ensuring your pantry is stocked with nutritious essentials. Here are some practical tips to help you shop on a budget without compromising on quality or nutrition.

First and foremost, planning is key. Before heading to the store, take inventory of what you already have. This prevents you from buying duplicates and ensures you use up what you have before it goes bad. Create a meal plan for the week, focusing on recipes that use similar ingredients. This not only reduces waste but also maximizes the use of your purchases. From this meal plan, make a detailed shopping list and stick to it. Impulse buys can quickly add up, so having a list helps you stay focused and within budget.

Buying in bulk is a great way to save money, especially for staple items like grains, beans, and spices. These items have a long shelf life and can be stored easily. Many stores offer bulk bins where you can buy as much or as little as you need, which is not only economical but also reduces packaging waste. When buying perishable items like fruits and vegetables, choose those that are in season. Seasonal produce is often cheaper and fresher. Local farmers' markets are a great place to find seasonal produce at lower prices than grocery stores.

Don't overlook the frozen food aisle. Frozen fruits and vegetables are often cheaper than fresh ones and have a long shelf life. They are picked at peak ripeness and flash-frozen, which preserves their nutritional value. Frozen produce is a convenient and cost-effective way to ensure you always have healthy options on hand. Canned goods are another budget-friendly option. Look for canned beans, tomatoes, and fruits packed in their own juice or water rather than syrup. These items are versatile and can be used in a variety of dishes, from soups and stews to salads and side dishes.

Opting for store brands instead of name brands can also lead to significant savings. Store brands often offer the same quality as name brands but at a lower price. Compare the ingredients and nutritional information to make sure you're getting the best value for your money. Coupons and loyalty programs can further reduce your grocery bill. Many stores offer digital coupons that can be loaded onto your loyalty card. Additionally, some stores have apps that provide exclusive discounts and promotions.

Reducing meat consumption can also be beneficial for your wallet. Plant-based proteins like beans, lentils, and tofu are generally cheaper than meat and can be just as satisfying. Incorporate more vegetarian meals into your diet to cut costs without sacrificing nutrition. When buying meat, look for sales and stock up when prices are low. You can freeze portions to use later, ensuring you always have a protein source on hand without paying full price.

Lastly, consider making some items at home rather than buying pre-packaged versions. Homemade dressings, sauces, and snacks are often cheaper and healthier than store-bought versions. Plus, you have control over the ingredients, which allows you to avoid added sugars and preservatives.

In summary, eating healthily on a budget is entirely possible with a bit of planning and smart shopping strategies. By taking advantage of bulk buying, seasonal produce, store brands, and homemade options, you can keep your grocery bill low while ensuring you have all the essentials for nutritious meals. These budget-friendly tips not only help you save money but also encourage a more mindful and sustainable approach to shopping and eating.

## *3.3 Reading and Understanding Food Labels*

Navigating the grocery store aisles can be daunting, especially when faced with the myriad of food products claiming various health benefits. Understanding how to read and interpret food labels is a crucial skill for making informed choices and maintaining a healthy diet. Here, we break down the key components of food labels and provide tips on what to look for to ensure you are selecting the best options for your dietary needs.

The Nutrition Facts panel is the first place to start. This panel provides a wealth of information about the nutritional content of the food. Key elements to focus on include serving size, calories, and the amounts of various nutrients. Serving size is crucial because all the information on the label is based on this amount. Be mindful of the serving size and compare it to the amount you actually eat. If you consume more than the serving size listed, you will need to adjust the nutritional information accordingly.

Calories provide a measure of how much energy you get from a serving of this food. While it's important to be aware of the calorie content, also consider the quality of those calories. Focus on nutrient-dense foods that provide vitamins, minerals, and other beneficial nutrients rather than empty calories from sugars and fats.

The label also lists the amounts of macronutrients: fats, carbohydrates, and proteins. Look for foods with healthy fats, such as those from nuts, seeds, and avocados, and limit saturated and trans fats. Carbohydrates should ideally come from whole grains, fruits, and vegetables, which are higher in fiber and nutrients. Pay attention to added sugars, which are often listed under carbohydrates. Aim to minimize foods with high amounts of added sugars, as they can contribute to weight gain and other health issues.

Protein is essential for maintaining muscle mass and overall health. Ensure that your diet includes sufficient protein from both animal and plant sources. The label also includes information on dietary fiber, which is crucial for digestive health. High-fiber foods help to keep you full and support a healthy gut microbiome.

The % Daily Value (%DV) is another important element of the Nutrition Facts panel. It shows how much of each nutrient one serving of the food provides in the context of a daily diet. The %DV helps you determine if a serving of food is high or low in a nutrient. For example, a %DV of 5% or less is considered low, while 20% or more is considered high. Use these values to choose foods that are higher in vitamins, minerals, and fiber, and lower in saturated fat, sodium, and added sugars.

Ingredients lists are also crucial for understanding what is in your food. Ingredients are listed in descending order by weight, meaning the first few ingredients make up the bulk of the product. Look for foods with whole, recognizable ingredients and avoid those with long lists of unpronounceable additives and preservatives. Be particularly mindful of added sugars, which can appear under various names such as high fructose corn syrup, sucrose, and maltose.

Understanding food labels also involves recognizing marketing claims. Terms like “natural,” “organic,” “non-GMO,” and “whole grain” can be misleading. For example, “natural” does not necessarily mean the product is healthy or free of additives. “Organic” products are grown without synthetic pesticides or fertilizers, but they can still be high in sugars or fats. “Whole grain” products should list a whole grain as the first ingredient, but not all products labeled as such are 100% whole grain.

1

# CHAPTER 4
# MEAL PLANNING MASTERY

## *4.1 Planning Your Weekly Meals*

The cornerstone of a successful dietary regimen lies in meticulous meal planning. Taking the time to plan your weekly meals not only ensures that you adhere to your nutritional goals but also simplifies the cooking process, reduces food waste, and saves money. Here, we delve into the essentials of effective meal planning and offer practical tips to help you master this crucial skill.

Start by setting aside a dedicated time each week for meal planning. This could be a quiet Sunday afternoon or a convenient weekday evening. Use this time to reflect on the upcoming week, considering factors such as your schedule, family commitments, and any social events that may affect your meals. Planning ahead allows you to anticipate busy days and prepare accordingly, ensuring you have nutritious options available even when time is limited.

Begin your meal planning by selecting a variety of recipes that align with your dietary preferences and nutritional goals. Aim for a balance of proteins, carbohydrates, and healthy fats, incorporating a wide range of fruits, vegetables, lean proteins, and whole grains. Variety is key to preventing boredom and ensuring you receive a broad spectrum of nutrients. Look for recipes that are simple, quick, and use common ingredients to streamline your grocery shopping and cooking process.

Once you have chosen your recipes, create a detailed shopping list. Organize your list by categories such as produce, dairy, proteins, and pantry staples. This not only makes your shopping trip more efficient but also helps ensure you don't forget any essential items. As you shop, be mindful of seasonal produce and sales to make cost-effective choices.

Batch cooking is an invaluable technique for meal planning. Prepare larger quantities of staple items such as grains, legumes, and proteins that can be used throughout the week. For example, cook a big pot of quinoa or brown rice, roast a tray of mixed vegetables, and grill a few chicken breasts or tofu slices. These components can be mixed and matched to create different meals, reducing the time spent cooking each day. Portion out these items into containers, so they are ready to grab and go, making meal assembly quick and convenient.

Incorporate a variety of meal types into your plan to keep things interesting. Include options such as salads, stir-fries, soups, and casseroles, which can be easily customized with different ingredients and flavors. Consider theme nights, like Meatless Monday or Taco Tuesday, to add a fun and structured element to your week. These themes can inspire creativity and provide a sense of routine, making meal planning more enjoyable.

Flexibility is also an important aspect of meal planning. While having a plan is essential, it's equally important to be adaptable. Life is unpredictable, and there may be times when you need to adjust your plan. Keep a few versatile ingredients on hand, such as eggs, canned beans, and frozen vegetables, which can be quickly transformed into a meal in a pinch. This flexibility ensures that you can stick to your nutritional goals even when unexpected situations arise.

Don't forget to plan for snacks and beverages. Healthy snacks such as fruit, nuts, and yogurt can help keep your energy levels stable throughout the day. Plan to prepare and portion these snacks in advance to avoid reaching for less nutritious options. Similarly, consider your beverage choices, opting for water, herbal teas, and infused water over sugary drinks.

## *4.2 Time-Saving Cooking Techniques*

In today's fast-paced world, finding efficient ways to prepare nutritious meals is essential. Time-saving cooking techniques not only streamline the process but also ensure that you can enjoy healthy, home-cooked meals even on the busiest of days. Here, we explore various methods to help you maximize your time in the kitchen without compromising on quality or flavor.

Batch cooking, as mentioned earlier, is a cornerstone of time-saving strategies. By preparing large quantities of staple ingredients, you can reduce the daily burden of cooking. Spend a few hours on the weekend cooking grains, proteins, and vegetables that can be used throughout the week. Store these pre-cooked items in the refrigerator or freezer, portioned out into containers, so they are ready to be incorporated into meals. This approach not only saves time but also minimizes cleanup, as you only need to wash pots and pans once.

One-pot and one-pan meals are another effective technique for saving time. These recipes involve cooking all components of a meal in a single pot or pan, reducing the number of dishes you need to wash. Dishes like soups, stews, stir-fries, and sheet pan dinners are perfect examples. They are not only easy to prepare but also allow flavors to meld together, creating delicious and cohesive meals. Invest in a high-quality Dutch oven, sheet pan, or large skillet to make these meals with ease.

The use of kitchen appliances can significantly cut down on cooking time. Slow cookers and pressure cookers are particularly valuable. A slow cooker allows you to set it and forget it, cooking meals slowly over several hours while you go about your day. This is perfect for stews, chili, and casseroles. On the other hand, a pressure cooker can achieve similar results in a fraction of the time. It's ideal for cooking beans, grains, and tough cuts of meat quickly and efficiently. These appliances also retain more nutrients due to their gentle cooking methods.

Meal prepping is another powerful technique. Dedicate time once or twice a week to prepare ingredients for upcoming meals. Wash and chop vegetables, marinate proteins, and cook grains in advance. Store these prepped ingredients in airtight containers, making it easy to assemble meals quickly. For example, having pre-chopped vegetables means you can throw together a salad or stir-fry in minutes. Marinated proteins can be quickly grilled or baked, and pre-cooked grains can be reheated or added to soups and salads.

Utilize shortcuts like pre-washed greens, frozen vegetables, and canned beans. These items are just as nutritious as their fresh counterparts and save significant prep time. Frozen vegetables are often flash-frozen at peak ripeness, retaining their nutritional value. Canned beans are a convenient source of protein and fiber, and pre-washed greens can be used straight from the bag for salads and sautés.

Another time-saving technique is to cook double or triple batches of recipes and freeze portions for later use. Soups, stews, casseroles, and even cooked grains can be frozen and reheated as needed. This ensures you always have a homemade meal on hand, reducing the temptation to opt for takeout or processed foods. Label and date your frozen meals to keep track of what you have and ensure you use them within a reasonable time frame.

Finally, consider incorporating quick-cooking techniques like stir-frying, broiling, and grilling. Stir-frying involves cooking ingredients quickly over high heat, preserving their texture and flavor. Broiling and grilling impart a delicious char and cook proteins and vegetables rapidly. These methods not only save time but also enhance the flavors of your dishes.

## 4.3 Storage and Food Safety Tips

Proper storage and food safety are critical components of maintaining a healthy kitchen. Ensuring that your ingredients and prepared meals are stored correctly not only extends their shelf life but also prevents foodborne illnesses. Here, we provide essential tips for effective storage and food safety to help you keep your kitchen organized and your food fresh.

First and foremost, understanding the different types of storage is crucial. Perishable items such as dairy, meat, and fresh produce should be stored in the refrigerator at temperatures below 40°F (4°C). Ensure that your refrigerator is clean and organized, with raw meats stored on the bottom shelf to prevent cross-contamination. Use clear, airtight containers to store leftovers and prepped ingredients. This not only keeps them fresh but also makes it easy to see what you have on hand.

Freezing is an excellent way to extend the shelf life of many foods. Most cooked meals, grains, vegetables, and proteins can be frozen for several months. Use freezer-safe containers or bags, and label them with the contents and date of freezing. This practice helps you keep track of what you have and ensures that you use items before they lose their quality. Thaw frozen foods safely by transferring them to the refrigerator or using the defrost function on your microwave, never at room temperature, to prevent bacterial growth.

Dry goods such as grains, legumes, and spices should be stored in a cool, dry place, preferably in airtight containers. This prevents exposure to moisture and pests, preserving their quality and flavor. Organize your pantry by grouping similar items together and using labels to easily identify contents. This organization not only makes it easier to find what you need but also helps you keep track of inventory, reducing the likelihood of buying duplicates or letting items go to waste.

Proper food handling is also essential for safety. Wash your hands thoroughly with soap and water before and after handling food, especially raw meat, poultry, and seafood. Use separate cutting boards for raw meats and vegetables to prevent cross-contamination. Ensure that all utensils, cutting boards, and countertops are cleaned with hot, soapy water after each use.

Cooking foods to the correct internal temperature is vital for food safety. Use a food thermometer to check that meats are cooked to the appropriate temperature: 165°F (74°C) for poultry, 160°F (71°C) for ground meats, and 145°F

(63°C) for whole cuts of beef, pork, and fish. Proper cooking kills harmful bacteria and reduces the risk of foodborne illnesses.

Leftovers should be cooled and stored promptly. Refrigerate or freeze leftovers within two hours of cooking to prevent bacterial growth. Divide large quantities of food into smaller portions to cool them faster. Consume refrigerated leftovers within three to four days, and reheat them to an internal temperature of 165°F (74°C) before eating. When in doubt, trust your senses: if a food item smells off or shows signs of spoilage, it’s best to discard it.

Another important aspect of food safety is understanding expiration dates. "Sell by" dates indicate how long a store should display the product, while "use by" or "best by" dates suggest when the product will be at its best quality. Foods are often still safe to eat after these dates if they have been stored properly, but always check for signs of spoilage. For highly perishable items like dairy and meats, it's best to adhere to the expiration dates closely.

# CHAPTER 5

# BREAKFASTS TO START YOUR DAY RIGHT

## *5.1 Quick Fixes for Busy Mornings*

### 1. Greek Yogurt with Fresh Fruit

**Introduction**:
Start your day with a delightful and nutritious breakfast that combines the creamy goodness of Greek yogurt with the fresh, sweet flavors of strawberries and kiwi. This simple yet satisfying dish is perfect for a quick morning meal, providing essential proteins and vitamins to energize your day.

**Ingredients for 1 serving**:
- 1 cup plain nonfat Greek yogurt
- 1/2 cup sliced strawberries
- 1/2 kiwi, peeled and sliced

**Preparation time**:- 5 minutes
**Cooking time**:- None

**Directions**:
1. Spoon the Greek yogurt into a serving bowl.
2. Arrange the sliced strawberries and kiwi on top of the yogurt.
3. Serve immediately and enjoy!

**Nutritional value per serving**:
- Calories: 120- Carbs: 15g- Fiber: 2g- Sugars: 10g- Protein: 13g- Saturated fat: 0g- Unsaturated fat: 0g

**Difficulty rating**:- ★☆☆☆☆

### 2. Hard-Boiled Eggs with Grape Tomatoes and Cucumber Slices

**Introduction**:
Hard-boiled eggs are a protein-packed, easy-to-prepare breakfast option. Paired with fresh grape tomatoes and cucumber slices, this dish provides a refreshing and balanced start to your day. It's perfect for those mornings when you need a quick, no-fuss meal.

**Ingredients for 1 serving**:
- 2 large eggs
- 1/2 cup grape tomatoes
- 1/2 cucumber, sliced

**Preparation time**:- 5 minutes
**Cooking time**:- 10 minutes

**Directions**:
1. Place the eggs in a saucepan and cover them with cold water.
2. Bring the water to a boil over medium-high heat.
3. Once the water reaches a rolling boil, turn off the heat, cover the saucepan, and let the eggs sit for 10 minutes.
4. While the eggs are cooking, wash the grape tomatoes and cucumber.
5. Slice the cucumber into rounds.
6. After 10 minutes, transfer the eggs to a bowl of ice water to cool for a few minutes.
7. Peel the eggs and serve them with the grape tomatoes and cucumber slices.

**Nutritional value per serving**:
- Calories: 150- Carbs: 6g- Fiber: 2g- Sugars: 4g- Protein: 12g- Saturated fat: 3g- Unsaturated fat: 2g

**Difficulty rating**:- ★☆☆☆☆

# 3. Apple Slices with Cinnamon

**Introduction**:
A simple yet delightful way to start your morning, these apple slices sprinkled with cinnamon offer a perfect blend of sweetness and spice. This dish not only satisfies your sweet tooth but also provides essential vitamins and fiber to kickstart your day.

**Ingredients for 1 serving**:
- 1 medium apple, thinly sliced
- 1/2 teaspoon ground cinnamon

**Preparation time**:- 5 minutes
**Cooking time**:- None

**Directions**:
1. Wash the apple thoroughly and pat dry.
2. Slice the apple into thin wedges, discarding the core.
3. Arrange the apple slices on a plate.
4. Sprinkle ground cinnamon evenly over the apple slices.
5. Serve immediately and enjoy the fresh, crisp flavors.

**Nutritional value per serving**:- Calories: 95- Carbs: 25g- Fiber: 4g- Sugars: 19g- Protein: 0.5g- Saturated fat: 0g- Unsaturated fat: 0g

**Difficulty rating**:- ★☆☆☆☆

## 4. Protein-Packed Smoothie

**Introduction**:
This smoothie is a powerhouse of nutrients, blending the creamy texture of Greek yogurt with the freshness of spinach and the sweetness of berries. Perfect for a quick breakfast or a post-workout snack, it's both refreshing and revitalizing.

**Ingredients for 1 serving**:
- 1/2 cup plain nonfat Greek yogurt
- 1 cup frozen spinach
- 1/2 cup mixed berries (strawberries, blueberries, raspberries)
- 1/2 cup water

**Preparation time**:- 5 minutes
**Cooking time**:- None

**Directions**:
1. Place the Greek yogurt, frozen spinach, mixed berries, and water into a blender.
2. Blend on high until the mixture is smooth and creamy.
3. Pour the smoothie into a glass.
4. Serve immediately and enjoy the nutritious blend.

**Nutritional value per serving**:- Calories: 130- Carbs: 22g- Fiber: 6g- Sugars: 13g- Protein: 10g- Saturated fat: 0g- Unsaturated fat: 0g

**Difficulty rating**:- ★☆☆☆☆

## 5. Banana Pancakes

**Introduction**:
Indulge in these deliciously simple banana pancakes, perfect for a quick and healthy breakfast. Made with just two ingredients, they are light, fluffy, and packed with natural sweetness from the banana. These pancakes are not only easy to prepare but also provide a satisfying start to your day.

**Ingredients for 1 serving**:
- 1 ripe banana
- 2 large eggs

**Preparation time**:- 5 minutes
**Cooking time**:- 5 minutes

**Directions**:
1. In a blender, combine the banana and eggs.
2. Blend until smooth.
3. Heat a non-stick skillet over medium heat.
4. Pour a small amount of batter onto the skillet to form pancakes.
5. Cook for 1-2 minutes on each side, or until golden brown.
6. Serve hot and enjoy!

**Nutritional value per serving**:
- Calories: 210- Carbs: 27g- Fiber: 3g- Sugars: 14g- Protein: 12g- Saturated fat: 2g- Unsaturated fat: 2g

**Difficulty rating**:- ★☆☆☆☆

## 6. Fruit Kebabs

**Introduction**:
These vibrant fruit kebabs are a refreshing and fun way to enjoy a variety of fresh fruits. Perfect for a light breakfast or snack, they are easy to prepare and visually appealing. The combination of pineapple, melon, and strawberries provides a burst of flavors and essential nutrients.

**Ingredients for 1 serving**:
- 4 pineapple chunks
- 4 melon chunks
- 4 strawberries, hulled

**Preparation time**:- 10 minutes
**Cooking time**:- None

**Directions**:
1. Wash and hull the strawberries.
2. Cut the pineapple and melon into bite-sized chunks.
3. Thread the fruit pieces onto skewers, alternating between pineapple, melon, and strawberries.
4. Serve immediately and enjoy!

**Nutritional value per serving**:
- Calories: 70- Carbs: 18g- Fiber: 2g- Sugars: 15g- Protein: 1g- Saturated fat: 0g- Unsaturated fat: 0g

**Difficulty rating**:- ★☆☆☆☆

## 7. Veggie Capsicum Cups

**Introduction:**
These vibrant veggie capsicum cups are not only visually appealing but also packed with nutrients. Bell peppers serve as an edible bowl, filled with a delicious mixture of scrambled egg whites and spinach. This low-calorie breakfast option is perfect for starting your day on a healthy note.

**Ingredients for 1 serving:**
- 1 medium bell pepper, halved and seeded
- 1/2 cup egg whites
- 1/2 cup fresh spinach, chopped
- Salt and pepper to taste

**Preparation time:**- 10 minutes
**Cooking time:**- 15 minutes

**Directions:**
1. Preheat the oven to 375°F (190°C).
2. Cut the bell pepper in half and remove the seeds.
3. Place the pepper halves on a baking sheet.

4. In a bowl, whisk the egg whites and season with salt and pepper.
5. Add the chopped spinach to the egg whites and mix well.
6. Pour the egg mixture into the bell pepper halves.
7. Bake in the preheated oven for 15 minutes or until the eggs are set.
8. Serve hot and enjoy!

**Nutritional value per serving:**
- Calories: 80- Carbs: 6g- Fiber: 2g- Sugars: 4g- Protein: 10g- Saturated fat: 0g- Unsaturated fat: 0g

Difficulty rating:- ★☆☆☆☆

# 8. Cold Turkey Roll-Ups

**Introduction:**
Cold turkey roll-ups are a quick and easy breakfast or snack option that combines the lean protein of turkey breast with the crisp freshness of lettuce and carrots. These roll-ups are perfect for a light and nutritious start to your day or as a portable snack on the go.

**Ingredients for 1 serving:**
- 3 slices of turkey breast
- 3 large lettuce leaves
- 1/2 cup shredded carrots

**Preparation time:**- 5 minutes
**Cooking time:**- None

**Directions:**
1. Lay out the turkey slices on a clean surface.
2. Place a lettuce leaf on top of each turkey slice.
3. Sprinkle shredded carrots evenly over the lettuce.
4. Roll up each turkey slice tightly.
5. Secure with a toothpick if needed.
6. Serve immediately and enjoy!

**Nutritional value per serving:**
- Calories: 90- Carbs: 4g- Fiber: 1g- Sugars: 2g- Protein: 16g- Saturated fat: 0.5g- Unsaturated fat: 0.5g

**Difficulty rating:**- ★☆☆☆☆

## *5.2 ENERGIZING BREAKFAST OPTIONS*

# 9. Mixed Berry Bowl

**Introduction:**
Kickstart your day with this vibrant Mixed Berry Bowl, combining the fresh sweetness of strawberries, blueberries, and raspberries with the creamy tang of nonfat yogurt. This delightful and nutritious breakfast is perfect for a refreshing morning boost, offering a plethora of vitamins and antioxidants.

**Ingredients for 1 serving:**
- 1/2 cup fresh strawberries, hulled and sliced
- 1/2 cup fresh blueberries
- 1/2 cup fresh raspberries
- 1/2 cup plain nonfat yogurt

**Preparation time:**- 5 minutes
**Cooking time:**- None

**Directions:**
1. Wash and hull the strawberries, then slice them.
2. Wash the blueberries and raspberries.
3. In a serving bowl, combine the strawberries, blueberries, and raspberries.
4. Add a dollop of plain nonfat yogurt on top of the mixed berries.
5. Serve immediately and enjoy!

**Nutritional value per serving:**
- Calories: 110- Carbs: 22g- Fiber: 6g- Sugars: 14g- Protein: 6g- Saturated fat: 0g- Unsaturated fat: 0g

**Difficulty rating:**- ★☆☆☆☆

# 10. Spicy Tomato Shakshuka

**Introduction:**
Experience a burst of Middle Eastern flavors with this Spicy Tomato Shakshuka. Eggs are poached in a rich, spicy tomato sauce infused with chili peppers, onions, cumin, and paprika. This hearty breakfast dish is both satisfying and packed with protein, making it a perfect way to start your day.

**Ingredients for 1 serving:**
- 2 large eggs
- 1 cup diced tomatoes
- 1/4 cup chopped onion
- 1/2 chili pepper, sliced
- 1/2 teaspoon ground cumin
- 1/2 teaspoon paprika
- Salt and pepper to taste
- Fresh cilantro for garnish

**Preparation time:**- 10 minutes

**Cooking time:**- 15 minutes

**Directions:**
1. Heat a non-stick skillet over medium heat.
2. Add the chopped onion and sliced chili pepper to the skillet and sauté until softened.
3. Stir in the diced tomatoes, cumin, paprika, salt, and pepper. Cook for 5 minutes, allowing the flavors to meld.
4. Create two small wells in the tomato mixture and crack an egg into each well.
5. Cover the skillet and cook for 7-10 minutes, or until the eggs are set to your desired doneness.
6. Garnish with fresh cilantro and serve hot.

**Nutritional value per serving:**
- Calories: 160- Carbs: 10g- Fiber: 3g- Sugars: 6g- Protein: 12g- Saturated fat: 3g- Unsaturated fat: 5g

**Difficulty rating:**- ★★☆☆☆

# 11. Turkey and Spinach Omelette

**Introduction:**
This Turkey and Spinach Omelette is a protein-packed breakfast that's both delicious and nutritious. The combination of eggs, turkey breast, and fresh spinach provides a hearty start to your day, ensuring you stay full and energized.

**Ingredients for 1 serving:**
- 2 large eggs
- 1/4 cup diced skinless turkey breast
- 1/2 cup fresh spinach, chopped
- Salt and pepper to taste

**Preparation time:**- 5 minutes
**Cooking time:**- 5 minutes

**Directions:**
1. In a bowl, whisk the eggs with a pinch of salt and pepper.
2. Heat a non-stick skillet over medium heat.
3. Add the diced turkey breast to the skillet and cook until lightly browned.
4. Add the chopped spinach to the skillet and sauté until wilted.
5. Pour the whisked eggs over the turkey and spinach mixture.
6. Cook until the edges begin to set, then gently lift the edges with a spatula to let uncooked egg flow underneath.
7. Once the eggs are fully set, fold the omelette in half and slide onto a plate.
8. Serve hot and enjoy!

**Nutritional value per serving:**
- Calories: 210- Carbs: 2g- Fiber: 1g- Sugars: 1g- Protein: 25g- Saturated fat: 3g- Unsaturated fat: 5g

**Difficulty rating:**- ★☆☆☆☆

# 12. Smoked Salmon and Cucumber Rolls

**Introduction:**
These elegant Smoked Salmon and Cucumber Rolls are a delightful and refreshing breakfast option. The thinly sliced cucumber wrapped around savory smoked salmon, garnished with fresh dill, creates a perfect balance of flavors and textures.

**Ingredients for 1 serving:**
- 4 thin slices of cucumber
- 2 ounces smoked salmon
- Fresh dill for garnish

**Preparation time:**- 5 minutes
**Cooking time:**- None

**Directions:**
1. Use a mandoline or vegetable peeler to slice the cucumber into thin strips.
2. Lay out the cucumber slices on a clean surface.
3. Place a small piece of smoked salmon on each cucumber slice.
4. Roll up the cucumber slices tightly around the smoked salmon.
5. Secure with a toothpick if necessary.
6. Garnish with fresh dill.
7. Serve immediately and enjoy!

**Nutritional value per serving:**
- Calories: 90- Carbs: 3g- Fiber: 1g- Sugars: 1g- Protein: 11g- Saturated fat: 1g- Unsaturated fat: 2g

**Difficulty rating:**- ★☆☆☆☆

# 13. Fruit Smoothie

**Introduction:**
Start your day with this refreshing and nutritious fruit smoothie, packed with the natural sweetness of mixed berries and bananas. This smoothie is perfect for a quick breakfast or a revitalizing snack, offering a delicious way to enjoy a variety of fruits.

**Ingredients for 1 serving:**
- 1/2 cup frozen mixed berries (strawberries, blueberries, raspberries)
- 1 medium banana
- 1/2 cup water

**Preparation time:**- 5 minutes
**Cooking time:**- None

**Directions:**
1. Place the frozen mixed berries, banana, and water into a blender.
2. Blend on high until smooth and creamy.
3. Pour the smoothie into a glass.
4. Serve immediately and enjoy!

**Nutritional value per serving:**
- Calories: 120- Carbs: 30g- Fiber: 5g- Sugars: 20g- Protein: 1g- Saturated fat: 0g- Unsaturated fat: 0g

**Difficulty rating:**- ★☆☆☆☆

# 14. Grilled Chicken Salad

**Introduction:**
This Grilled Chicken Salad is a refreshing and nutritious breakfast option, perfect for those who prefer a savory start to their day. The combination of lean chicken breast, mixed greens, cucumbers, and tomatoes provides a balanced and satisfying meal.

**Ingredients for 1 serving:**
- 1 cup mixed greens
- 1/2 cup sliced cucumber
- 1/2 cup cherry tomatoes, halved
- 4 ounces skinless chicken breast
- Salt and pepper to taste
- Fresh lemon juice (optional)

**Preparation time:**- 10 minutes
**Cooking time:**- 10 minutes
**Directions:**
1. Preheat a grill or grill pan over medium heat.
2. Season the chicken breast with salt and pepper.
3. Grill the chicken breast for about 5 minutes on each side, or until fully cooked.
4. While the chicken is grilling, arrange the mixed greens, sliced cucumber, and cherry tomatoes on a plate.
5. Once the chicken is cooked, let it rest for a few minutes before chopping it into bite-sized pieces.
6. Add the chopped chicken to the salad.
7. Drizzle with fresh lemon juice if desired.
8. Serve immediately and enjoy!

**Nutritional value per serving:**
- Calories: 220- Carbs: 6g- Fiber: 2g- Sugars: 3g- Protein: 30g- Saturated fat: 1g- Unsaturated fat: 2g

**Difficulty rating:**- ★☆☆☆☆

# 14. Salsa Egg Muffins

**Introduction:**
Salsa Egg Muffins are a convenient and tasty breakfast option that can be made ahead of time. Packed with protein and veggies, these muffins are perfect for busy mornings. The combination of eggs, salsa, onions, and green peppers creates a flavorful and satisfying meal.

**Ingredients for 1 serving:**
- 2 large eggs
- 1/4 cup salsa
- 2 tablespoons diced onions
- 2 tablespoons diced green peppers
- Salt and pepper to taste

**Preparation time:**- 10 minutes
**Cooking time:**- 20 minutes

**Directions:**
1. Preheat the oven to 350°F (175°C).
2. In a bowl, whisk the eggs with salt and pepper.
3. Add the salsa, diced onions, and green peppers to the egg mixture and stir to combine.
4. Spray a muffin tin with non-stick cooking spray.
5. Pour the egg mixture into the muffin tin, filling each cup about 3/4 full.
6. Bake in the preheated oven for 20 minutes or until the eggs are set.
7. Let the muffins cool slightly before removing from the tin.
8. Serve warm and enjoy!

**Nutritional value per serving:**
- Calories: 120- Carbs: 4g- Fiber: 1g- Sugars: 2g- Protein: 10g- Saturated fat: 2g- Unsaturated fat: 3g

**Difficulty rating:**- ★☆☆☆☆

## 15. Tofu and Veggie Scramble

**Introduction:**
This Tofu and Veggie Scramble is a hearty and nutritious breakfast that's perfect for those looking to add more plant-based options to their diet. The combination of tofu and a variety of vegetables creates a delicious and satisfying meal that's easy to prepare.

**Ingredients for 1 serving:**
- 1/2 cup firm tofu, crumbled
- 1/4 cup chopped spinach
- 1/4 cup sliced mushrooms
- 1/4 cup diced tomatoes
- 1 clove garlic, minced
- 1 teaspoon olive oil
- Salt and pepper to taste

**Preparation time:**- 10 minutes
**Cooking time:**- 10 minutes

**Directions:**
1. Heat the olive oil in a non-stick skillet over medium heat.
2. Add the minced garlic and sauté for about 1 minute until fragrant.
3. Add the sliced mushrooms and cook until they start to soften.
4. Add the crumbled tofu, chopped spinach, and diced tomatoes to the skillet.
5. Cook, stirring frequently, until the vegetables are tender and the tofu is heated through.

6. Season with salt and pepper to taste.
7. Serve hot and enjoy!

**Nutritional value per serving:**
- Calories: 140- Carbs: 8g- Fiber: 3g- Sugars: 3g- Protein: 12g- Saturated fat: 1g- Unsaturated fat: 4g

**Difficulty rating:**- ★☆☆☆☆

## 5.3 *Weekend Brunch Favorites*

# 16. Egg and Spinach Casserole

**Introduction:**
This Egg and Spinach Casserole is a hearty and nutritious brunch option, perfect for weekends when you have a little more time to enjoy a leisurely meal. The combination of baked eggs, spinach, mushrooms, and tomatoes, seasoned with herbs, makes for a flavorful and satisfying dish.

**Ingredients for 1 serving:**
- 2 large eggs
- 1/2 cup fresh spinach, chopped
- 1/4 cup sliced mushrooms
- 1/4 cup diced tomatoes
- 1/4 teaspoon dried oregano
- Salt and pepper to taste

**Preparation time:**- 10 minutes
**Cooking time:**- 20 minutes

**Directions:**
1. Preheat the oven to 375°F (190°C).
2. In a bowl, whisk the eggs with salt, pepper, and dried oregano.
3. Spray a small baking dish with non-stick cooking spray.
4. Spread the chopped spinach, sliced mushrooms, and diced tomatoes evenly in the baking dish.
5. Pour the whisked eggs over the vegetables.
6. Bake in the preheated oven for 20 minutes or until the eggs are set.
7. Let the casserole cool slightly before serving.
8. Serve warm and enjoy!

**Nutritional value per serving:**
- Calories: 150- Carbs: 5g- Fiber: 2g- Sugars: 3g- Protein: 12g- Saturated fat: 3g- Unsaturated fat: 4g

**Difficulty rating:**- ★☆☆☆☆

# 17. Zucchini and Egg Frittata

**Introduction:**
This Zucchini and Egg Frittata is a delicious and nutritious brunch option, perfect for a relaxing weekend meal. The grated zucchini mixed with eggs and baked until set creates a light yet satisfying dish that's full of flavor.

**Ingredients for 1 serving:**
- 2 large eggs
- 1/2 cup grated zucchini
- 1/4 cup diced onions
- 1 clove garlic, minced
- 1 teaspoon olive oil
- Salt and pepper to taste

**Preparation time:**- 10 minutes
**Cooking time:**- 20 minutes

**Directions:**
1. Preheat the oven to 375°F (190°C).
2. Heat the olive oil in a non-stick skillet over medium heat.
3. Add the diced onions and minced garlic, and sauté until softened.
4. Add the grated zucchini to the skillet and cook for about 2 minutes until slightly tender.
5. In a bowl, whisk the eggs with salt and pepper.
6. Add the cooked vegetables to the eggs and stir to combine.
7. Pour the mixture into a small baking dish.
8. Bake in the preheated oven for 20 minutes or until the eggs are set.
9. Let the frittata cool slightly before serving.
10. Serve warm and enjoy!

**Nutritional value per serving:**
- Calories: 160- Carbs: 6g- Fiber: 2g- Sugars: 3g- Protein: 13g- Saturated fat: 3g- Unsaturated fat: 4g

**Difficulty rating:**- ★☆☆☆☆

# 18. Cantaloupe and Berry Salad

**Introduction:**
This Cantaloupe and Berry Salad is a refreshing and vibrant brunch option, perfect for a warm weekend morning. The sweet cantaloupe paired with tangy blueberries and raspberries, all drizzled with lemon juice, creates a delightful and nutritious dish.

**Ingredients for 1 serving:**
- 1 cup fresh cantaloupe, cubed
- 1/2 cup fresh blueberries
- 1/2 cup fresh raspberries
- 1 tablespoon fresh lemon juice

**Preparation time:**- 10 minutes
**Cooking time:**- None

**Directions:**
1. In a large bowl, combine the cantaloupe cubes, blueberries, and raspberries.
2. Drizzle the fresh lemon juice over the fruit.
3. Toss gently to combine all the ingredients evenly.
4. Serve immediately or chill in the refrigerator for a few minutes before serving.
5. Enjoy this refreshing salad as a light and healthy brunch option.

**Nutritional value per serving:**
- Calories: 80- Carbs: 20g Fiber: 4g- Sugars: 14g- Protein: 1g- Saturated fat: 0g- Unsaturated fat: 0g

**Difficulty rating:**- ★☆☆☆☆

## 19. Seafood Salad

**Introduction:**
This Seafood Salad is a light yet satisfying brunch option, featuring mixed greens topped with succulent shrimp and scallops, all dressed with a zesty lemon and herb dressing. It's a perfect way to enjoy a gourmet meal at home.

**Ingredients for 1 serving:**
- 1 cup mixed greens
- 3 ounces cooked shrimp
- 3 ounces cooked scallops
- 1 tablespoon fresh lemon juice
- 1 teaspoon olive oil
- 1 tablespoon fresh herbs (such as dill, parsley, or cilantro), chopped
- Salt and pepper to taste

**Preparation time**:- 10 minutes
**Cooking time:**- 5 minutes (for seafood, if not pre-cooked)

**Directions:**
1. If using raw shrimp and scallops, cook them in a skillet over medium heat with a teaspoon of olive oil until fully cooked, about 2-3 minutes per side.
2. In a large bowl, combine the mixed greens, cooked shrimp, and scallops.
3. In a small bowl, whisk together the lemon juice, olive oil, chopped herbs, salt, and pepper to make the dressing.
4. Drizzle the dressing over the salad and toss gently to combine.
5. Serve immediately and enjoy this delightful seafood salad as a nutritious brunch option.

**Nutritional value per serving:**
- Calories: 180- Carbs: 5g- Fiber: 2g- Sugars: 2g- Protein: 24g- Saturated fat: 1g- Unsaturated fat: 5g

**Difficulty rating:**- ★☆☆☆☆

## 20. Poached Eggs over Asparagus

**Introduction:**
Poached Eggs over Asparagus is a delightful brunch option that combines the earthy flavors of fresh asparagus with the richness of poached eggs. This dish is light yet satisfying, making it perfect for a weekend brunch.

**Ingredients for 1 serving:**
- 1/2 bunch fresh asparagus spears, trimmed
- 2 large eggs
- 1 tablespoon white vinegar
- 1/4 teaspoon salt
- 1/4 teaspoon black pepper
- Fresh herbs (such as chives or parsley) for garnish

**Preparation time:**- 10 minutes
**Cooking time:**- 10 minutes

**Directions:**
1. Bring a large pot of water to a boil and add a pinch of salt.
2. Add the asparagus spears and cook for 2-3 minutes until tender-crisp. Remove and set aside.
3. In a separate pot, bring water to a gentle simmer and add the white vinegar.
4. Crack each egg into a small bowl. Gently slide each egg into the simmering water.
5. Poach the eggs for about 3-4 minutes, or until the whites are set and the yolks are still runny.
6. Remove the eggs with a slotted spoon and drain on paper towels.
7. Arrange the asparagus on a plate, top with the poached eggs, and sprinkle with salt, pepper, and fresh herbs.
8. Serve immediately and enjoy!

**Nutritional value per serving:**
- Calories: 140- Carbs: 6g- Fiber: 3g- Sugars: 3g- Protein: 12g- Saturated fat: 3g- Unsaturated fat: 4g

**Difficulty rating:**- ★☆☆☆☆

# 21. Mixed Vegetable Soup

**Introduction:**
Mixed Vegetable Soup is a nutritious and warming dish, perfect for a weekend brunch. This puree of zero-point vegetables like tomatoes, celery, and carrots is seasoned to taste and provides a burst of flavors in every spoonful.

**Ingredients for 1 serving:**
- 1 cup tomatoes, chopped
- 1/2 cup celery, chopped
- 1/2 cup carrots, chopped
- 1/4 cup onions, chopped
- 1 clove garlic, minced
- 1 teaspoon olive oil
- 1 cup vegetable broth
- Salt and pepper to taste
- Fresh herbs (such as basil or thyme) for garnish

**Preparation time:**- 10 minutes
**Cooking time:**- 20 minutes

**Directions:**
1. Heat the olive oil in a large pot over medium heat.
2. Add the onions and garlic, and sauté until softened.
3. Add the tomatoes, celery, and carrots, and cook for about 5 minutes, stirring occasionally.
4. Pour in the vegetable broth and bring the mixture to a boil.
5. Reduce the heat and let it simmer for about 15 minutes, or until the vegetables are tender.
6. Use an immersion blender to puree the soup until smooth. Alternatively, transfer the soup to a blender in batches and blend until smooth.
7. Season with salt and pepper to taste.
8. Garnish with fresh herbs and serve hot.

**Nutritional value per serving:**
- Calories: 90- Carbs: 18g- Fiber: 4g- Sugars: 10g- Protein: 2g- Saturated fat: 1g- Unsaturated fat: 2g

**Difficulty rating:**- ★☆☆☆☆

## 22. Herbed Chicken Skewers

**Introduction:**
Herbed Chicken Skewers are a flavorful and satisfying brunch option. The skinless chicken breast pieces are marinated in a blend of fresh herbs and spices, then grilled to perfection. This dish is both healthy and delicious, making it a perfect addition to your weekend brunch menu.

**Ingredients for 1 serving:**
- 4 ounces skinless chicken breast, cut into bite-sized pieces
- 1 tablespoon olive oil
- 1 tablespoon fresh lemon juice
- 1 clove garlic, minced
- 1 tablespoon fresh parsley, chopped
- 1 tablespoon fresh thyme, chopped
- 1/2 teaspoon salt
- 1/4 teaspoon black pepper
- Skewers (if using wooden skewers, soak in water for 30 minutes before use)

**Preparation time:**- 10 minutes
**Cooking time:**- 10 minutes (plus 30 minutes marinating time)

**Directions:**
1. In a bowl, combine the olive oil, lemon juice, garlic, parsley, thyme, salt, and pepper.
2. Add the chicken pieces to the marinade and toss to coat evenly. Cover and refrigerate for at least 30 minutes.
3. Preheat the grill to medium-high heat.
4. Thread the marinated chicken pieces onto the skewers.
5. Grill the chicken skewers for about 4-5 minutes on each side, or until the chicken is cooked through and has nice grill marks.
6. Remove from the grill and let rest for a few minutes before serving.
7. Serve immediately and enjoy these flavorful Herbed Chicken Skewers.

**Nutritional value per serving:**
- Calories: 200- Carbs: 1g- Fiber: 0g- Sugars: 0g- Protein: 26g- Saturated fat: 1g- Unsaturated fat: 6g

**Difficulty rating:**- ★☆☆☆☆

## 23. Cucumber and Yogurt Soup

**Introduction:**
Cucumber and Yogurt Soup is a refreshing and light dish perfect for a weekend brunch. This chilled soup blends the crispness of cucumber with the creaminess of plain nonfat yogurt, enhanced with dill and garlic for added flavor.

**Ingredients for 1 serving:**
- 1 cup cucumber, peeled and chopped
- 1 cup plain nonfat Greek yogurt
- 1 clove garlic, minced
- 1 tablespoon fresh dill, chopped
- 1 tablespoon fresh lemon juice
- Salt and pepper to taste

**Preparation time:-** 10 minutes
**Cooking time:-** None

**Directions:**
1. In a blender, combine the cucumber, Greek yogurt, garlic, dill, and lemon juice.
2. Blend until smooth and creamy.
3. Season with salt and pepper to taste.
4. Chill the soup in the refrigerator for at least 30 minutes before serving.
5. Pour into a bowl and garnish with additional fresh dill if desired.
6. Serve cold and enjoy this refreshing Cucumber and Yogurt Soup.

**Nutritional value per serving:**
- Calories: 90- Carbs: 10g- Fiber: 1g- Sugars: 7g- Protein: 11g- Saturated fat: 0g- Unsaturated fat: 0g

**Difficulty rating:-** ★☆☆☆☆

# 24. Tomato and Basil Bruschetta

**Introduction:**
Tomato and Basil Bruschetta is a delightful and fresh dish perfect for a weekend brunch. The combination of ripe tomatoes and aromatic basil served over grilled eggplant slices provides a satisfying, healthy option that is both simple and delicious.

**Ingredients for 1 serving:**
- 1 medium eggplant, sliced
- 1 cup cherry tomatoes, chopped
- 2 tablespoons fresh basil, chopped
- 1 clove garlic, minced
- 1 tablespoon balsamic vinegar
- Salt and pepper to taste

**Preparation time:-** 10 minutes
**Cooking time:-** 10 minutes

**Directions:**
1. Preheat the grill to medium-high heat.
2. Lightly season the eggplant slices with salt and pepper.
3. Grill the eggplant slices for about 3-4 minutes on each side until tender and slightly charred.
4. In a bowl, combine the chopped tomatoes, basil, garlic, and balsamic vinegar. Mix well and season with salt and pepper to taste.
5. Place the grilled eggplant slices on a plate and top with the tomato-basil mixture.
6. Serve immediately and enjoy this fresh and flavorful Tomato and Basil Bruschetta.

**Nutritional value per serving:**
- Calories: 90- Carbs: 14g- Fiber: 6g- Sugars: 7g- Protein: 3g- Saturated fat: 0g- Unsaturated fat: 1g

**Difficulty rating:-** ★☆☆☆☆

# 25. Vegan Berry Parfait

**Introduction:**
Vegan Berry Parfait is a light and refreshing brunch option that combines layers of mixed berries with plain nonfat yogurt. This parfait is not only visually appealing but also packed with antioxidants and nutrients.

**Ingredients for 1 serving:**
- 1/2 cup strawberries, sliced
- 1/2 cup blueberries
- 1/2 cup raspberries
- 1 cup plain nonfat Greek yogurt
- 1 teaspoon honey (optional)
- Mint leaves for garnish (optional)

**Preparation time:**- 5 minutes
**Cooking time:**- None

**Directions:**
1. In a glass or bowl, start by layering 1/3 of the yogurt at the bottom.
2. Add a layer of mixed berries (strawberries, blueberries, and raspberries).
3. Repeat the layering process two more times, ending with a layer of berries on top.
4. Drizzle with honey if desired.
5. Garnish with mint leaves for an extra touch of freshness.
6. Serve immediately and enjoy this nutritious and delicious Vegan Berry Parfait.

**Nutritional value per serving:**
- Calories: 150- Carbs: 27g- Fiber: 5g- Sugars: 17g- Protein: 14g- Saturated fat: 0g- Unsaturated fat: 0g

**Difficulty rating:**- ★☆☆☆☆

# CHAPTER 6

# SATISFYING LUNCHES

## *6.1 Easy Pack-and-Go Lunches*

## 26. Chicken and Veggie Wrap

**Introduction:**
This Chicken and Veggie Wrap is perfect for a quick, healthy lunch on the go. Packed with lean protein and fresh vegetables, it's a flavorful and satisfying option that requires minimal preparation.

**Ingredients for 1 serving:**
- 4 oz grilled skinless chicken breast, sliced
- 1 large lettuce leaf (iceberg or romaine)
- 1/4 cup shredded carrots
- 1/4 cup sliced bell peppers
- 1/4 cup cucumber slices
- 1 tbsp hummus (optional for added flavor)
- Salt and pepper to taste

**Preparation time**: 10 minutes
**Cooking time**: 10 minutes (for grilling chicken)

**Directions:**
1. Prepare the Chicken: Grill the chicken breast if not pre-cooked. Season with salt and pepper.
2. Assemble the Wrap: Lay the lettuce leaf flat and spread a thin layer of hummus if using. Place sliced chicken, carrots, bell peppers, and cucumbers in the center of the lettuce leaf.
3. Wrap and Secure: Roll the lettuce leaf around the filling, securing it with a toothpick if necessary.

**Nutritional value per serving:**
- Calories: 150- Carbs: 10g- Fiber: 3g- Sugars: 3g- Protein: 24g- Saturated Fat: 0.5g- Unsaturated Fat: 1.5g

**Difficulty rating**: ★☆☆☆☆

## 27. Shrimp and Mango Salad

**Introduction:**
This refreshing Shrimp and Mango Salad combines the sweetness of mango with the savory taste of shrimp. It's light, flavorful, and perfect for a midday meal that's both nutritious and delicious.

**Ingredients for 1 serving:**
- 3 oz cooked shrimp, peeled and deveined
- 1/2 cup diced mango
- 1/4 cup cucumber, diced
- 1 tbsp red onion, finely chopped
- 1 tbsp fresh cilantro, chopped
- Juice of 1 lime
- Salt and pepper to taste

**Preparation time**: 15 minutes
**Cooking time**: 5 minutes (for cooking shrimp if needed)

**Directions:**
1. Prepare the Shrimp: If shrimp are not pre-cooked, boil or grill them until fully cooked and pink. Let cool.
2. Combine Ingredients: In a mixing bowl, combine the shrimp, mango, cucumber, red onion, and cilantro.
3. Dress the Salad: Squeeze lime juice over the mixture and toss gently to combine. Season with salt and pepper to taste.

**Nutritional value per serving:**
- Calories: 180- Carbs: 20g- Fiber: 3g- Sugars: 15g- Protein: 18g- Saturated Fat: 0g- Unsaturated Fat: 1g

**Difficulty rating**: ★☆☆☆☆

## 28. Turkey Lettuce Cups

**Introduction:**
Turkey Lettuce Cups are a fantastic low-carb, high-protein lunch option. They are quick to prepare and can be customized with various spices and vegetables to suit your taste.

**Ingredients for 1 serving:**
- 4 oz ground turkey breast
- 1/4 cup diced tomatoes
- 1/4 cup diced onions
- 1/4 cup diced bell peppers (optional)
- 2 large iceberg lettuce leaves
- 1/2 tsp chili powder
- 1/2 tsp cumin
- Salt and pepper to taste

**Preparation time**: 10 minutes
**Cooking time**: 10 minutes

**Directions:**
1. Cook the Turkey: In a nonstick skillet, cook the ground turkey over medium heat until browned, breaking it apart with a spoon.
2. Add Vegetables: Add diced tomatoes, onions, and bell peppers (if using) to the skillet. Stir in chili powder, cumin, salt, and pepper. Cook for an additional 5 minutes until vegetables are softened.
3. Assemble the Cups: Spoon the turkey mixture into the iceberg lettuce leaves. Serve immediately or pack for a convenient lunch.

**Nutritional value per serving:**
- Calories: 150- Carbs: 5g- Fiber: 2g- Sugars: 3g- Protein: 20g- Saturated Fat: 1g- Unsaturated Fat: 1g

**Difficulty rating**: ★☆☆☆☆

# 29. Vegetable Soup

**Introduction:**
This Vegetable Soup is a light yet nourishing dish perfect for lunch. Made with a variety of fresh vegetables, it's both flavorful and packed with nutrients.

**Ingredients for 1 serving:**
- 1/2 cup carrots, diced
- 1/2 cup celery, diced
- 1/2 cup onions, diced
- 1/2 cup spinach leaves
- 2 cups vegetable broth (low sodium)
- 1 clove garlic, minced
- 1/4 tsp dried thyme
- 1/4 tsp black pepper
- Salt to taste

**Preparation time**: 10 minutes
**Cooking time**: 20 minutes

**Directions:**
1. Sauté Vegetables: In a large pot, sauté the carrots, celery, and onions with minced garlic over medium heat until softened, about 5 minutes.
2. Add Broth and Seasoning: Add the vegetable broth, thyme, black pepper, and salt. Bring to a boil, then reduce heat and simmer for 15 minutes.
3. Add Spinach: Stir in the spinach leaves and cook for an additional 2 minutes until wilted.
4. Serve: Ladle the soup into bowls and enjoy hot.

**Nutritional value per serving:**
- Calories: 60- Carbs: 10g- Fiber: 3g- Sugars: 4g- Protein: 2g- Saturated Fat: 0g- Unsaturated Fat: 0g

**Difficulty rating**: ★☆☆☆☆

# 30. Egg Salad

**Introduction:**
This Egg Salad offers a creamy, protein-packed option perfect for lunch. It's a lighter take on the classic dish, using Greek yogurt instead of mayonnaise, and is easily portable for those on the go.

**Ingredients for 1 serving:**
- 2 large hard-boiled eggs, chopped
- 1/4 cup plain nonfat Greek yogurt
- 1 tbsp diced onions
- 1/2 tsp dried dill

- Salt and pepper to taste
- Lettuce leaves (optional, for wrapping)

**Preparation time:** 10 minutes
**Cooking time:** None (pre-cooked eggs)

**Directions:**
1. Prepare the Salad: In a bowl, combine the chopped eggs, Greek yogurt, and diced onions.
2. Season: Add dill, salt, and pepper. Mix well until the ingredients are evenly combined.
3. Serve: Enjoy as is, or wrap in lettuce leaves for a refreshing, crunchy bite.

**Nutritional value per serving:**
- Calories: 130- Carbs: 2g- Fiber: 0g- Sugars: 1g- Protein: 14g- Saturated Fat: 3g- Unsaturated Fat: 1g

**Difficulty rating**: ★☆☆☆☆

## 31. Spicy Bean Chili

**Introduction:**
This Spicy Bean Chili is a hearty and warming dish, perfect for a satisfying lunch. Packed with beans and tomatoes, it's rich in fiber and protein, offering a filling meal that's easy to take on the go.

**Ingredients for 1 serving:**
- 1/2 cup black beans, cooked
- 1/2 cup kidney beans, cooked
- 1/2 cup diced tomatoes
- 1/4 cup diced onions
- 1 clove garlic, minced
- 1/2 tsp chili powder
- 1/4 tsp cumin
- Salt to taste

**Preparation time**: 10 minutes
**Cooking time**: 20 minutes

**Directions:**
1. Cook Onions and Garlic: In a pot, sauté the onions and garlic over medium heat until softened, about 5 minutes.
2. Add Beans and Tomatoes: Stir in the black beans, kidney beans, and diced tomatoes.
3. Season: Add chili powder, cumin, and salt. Mix well.
4. Simmer: Reduce the heat and let the chili simmer for about 15 minutes, allowing the flavors to meld.
5. Serve: Enjoy hot, or pack in a thermos for a warm, portable lunch.

**Nutritional value per serving:**
- Calories: 200- Carbs: 35g- Fiber: 10g- Sugars: 5g- Protein: 10g- Saturated Fat: 0g- Unsaturated Fat: 1g

**Difficulty rating**: ★☆☆☆☆

# 32. Veggie Nori Rolls

**Introduction:**
Veggie Nori Rolls are a light and nutritious option for a lunch that's easy to pack and enjoy on the go. These rolls are filled with fresh vegetables, offering a satisfying crunch and a burst of natural flavors, all wrapped in seaweed sheets for an added boost of minerals.

**Ingredients for 1 serving:**
- 1 sheet of nori (seaweed)
- 1/4 cup thinly sliced cucumbers
- 1/4 cup thinly sliced carrots
- 1/4 cup thinly sliced bell peppers (red or yellow)
- 1/4 avocado, thinly sliced (optional for added creaminess)

**Preparation time**: 10 minutes
**Cooking time**: None

**Directions:**
1. Prepare the Vegetables: Thinly slice the cucumbers, carrots, and bell peppers into strips.
2. Assemble the Rolls: Place the nori sheet on a flat surface. Arrange the vegetables in a line along one edge of the nori sheet.
3. Roll: Gently roll the nori over the vegetables, keeping it tight to form a roll. Use a little water to seal the end of the nori sheet.
4. Cut and Serve: Slice the roll into bite-sized pieces. Enjoy immediately or pack for later.

**Nutritional value per serving:**
- Calories: 70- Carbs: 10g- Fiber: 4g- Sugars: 3g- Protein: 2g- Saturated Fat: 0g- Unsaturated Fat: 1g

**Difficulty rating:** ★☆☆☆☆

# 33. Zesty Salsa Chicken

**Introduction:**
This Zesty Salsa Chicken offers a flavorful and refreshing twist to your lunch routine. Made with shredded chicken breast and fresh salsa, this dish is perfect served over salad greens for a light and satisfying meal.

**Ingredients for 1 serving:**
- 1/2 cup shredded chicken breast (cooked)
- 1/4 cup fresh salsa (tomatoes, onions, cilantro, jalapeños)
- 2 cups mixed salad greens (lettuce, spinach, arugula)
- 1/4 cup diced bell peppers (optional)
- 1/4 avocado, sliced (optional)

**Preparation time**: 15 minutes
**Cooking time**: None (using pre-cooked chicken)

**Directions:**
1. Prepare the Chicken: If not already done, cook and shred the chicken breast.
2. Mix with Salsa: In a bowl, combine the shredded chicken with fresh salsa, mixing well.
3. Serve: Place the salad greens on a plate or in a lunch container. Top with the chicken and salsa mixture.

4. Optional Additions: Add diced bell peppers and avocado slices for extra flavor and texture.

**Nutritional value per serving:**
- Calories: 150- Carbs: 7g- Fiber: 3g- Sugars: 4g- Protein: 25g- Saturated Fat: 0.5g- Unsaturated Fat: 3g

**Difficulty rating**: ★☆☆☆☆

## 34. Spicy Tofu Sticks

**Introduction:**
Spicy Tofu Sticks are a delightful way to enjoy a plant-based protein that's packed with flavor. Marinated in a hot sauce blend and baked to perfection, these tofu sticks offer a satisfying crunch and a spicy kick, perfect for a quick and easy lunch. Pair them with a side of celery sticks for a refreshing contrast.

**Ingredients for 1 serving:**
- 1/2 block of firm tofu, pressed and sliced into sticks
- 2 tablespoons hot sauce (check for no added sugars)
- 1 tablespoon low-sodium soy sauce
- 1 teaspoon olive oil
- 1/4 teaspoon garlic powder
- 1/4 teaspoon paprika
- 1 cup celery sticks

**Preparation time**: 10 minutes
**Cooking time**: 20 minutes

**Directions:**
1. Preheat the Oven: Preheat your oven to 375°F (190°C) and line a baking sheet with parchment paper.
2. Prepare the Tofu: Press the tofu to remove excess water, then slice into sticks.
3. Marinate the Tofu: In a bowl, mix the hot sauce, soy sauce, olive oil, garlic powder, and paprika. Toss the tofu sticks in the marinade until evenly coated. Let sit for 5 minutes to absorb flavors.
4. Bake the Tofu: Arrange the tofu sticks on the prepared baking sheet. Bake for 20 minutes, flipping halfway through, until the tofu is crispy and golden.
5. Serve: Serve the tofu sticks hot with a side of celery sticks for dipping or snacking.

**Nutritional value per serving:**
- Calories: 150- Carbs: 6g- Fiber: 3g- Sugars: 2g- Protein: 14g- Saturated Fat: 0.5g- Unsaturated Fat: 3g

**Difficulty rating**: ★☆☆☆☆

## 6.2 *QUICK HOME LUNCH IDEAS*

# 35. Tomato Basil Soup

**Introduction:**
Tomato Basil Soup is a classic and comforting dish, perfect for a quick and easy lunch at home. This recipe highlights the natural flavors of ripe tomatoes and fresh basil, resulting in a smooth and satisfying soup that's both nutritious and delicious.

**Ingredients for 1 serving:**
- 4 medium ripe tomatoes, chopped
- 1 cup vegetable broth (low-sodium)
- 1/4 cup fresh basil leaves, chopped
- 1 clove garlic, minced
- 1/2 teaspoon olive oil
- Salt and pepper to taste

**Preparation time**: 10 minutes
**Cooking time**: 20 minutes

**Directions:**
1. Sauté Garlic: In a medium saucepan, heat the olive oil over medium heat. Add the minced garlic and sauté for about 1 minute until fragrant.
2. Cook Tomatoes: Add the chopped tomatoes to the pan. Cook for about 5 minutes, stirring occasionally, until the tomatoes begin to break down.
3. Add Broth and Basil: Pour in the vegetable broth and add the chopped basil leaves. Bring the mixture to a boil, then reduce the heat and simmer for 10 minutes.
4. Blend the Soup: Use an immersion blender to puree the soup until smooth. If you prefer a chunkier texture, blend only a portion of the soup.
5. Season and Serve: Season with salt and pepper to taste. Serve hot, garnished with additional fresh basil if desired.

**Nutritional value per serving:**
- Calories: 120- Carbs: 18g- Fiber: 4g- Sugars: 9g- Protein: 2g- Saturated Fat: 0g- Unsaturated Fat: 1g

**Difficulty rating:** ★☆☆☆☆

# 36. Broccoli and Egg Frittata

**Introduction:**
This Broccoli and Egg Frittata is a quick and healthy lunch option that's perfect for those looking to enjoy a warm, home-cooked meal. Packed with protein and fiber, this dish is both filling and nutritious, making it an excellent choice for a balanced diet.

**Ingredients for 1 serving:**
- 2 large eggs
- 1 cup broccoli florets, steamed
- 1/4 cup onion, finely chopped
- 1/4 teaspoon olive oil

- Salt and pepper to taste
- Fresh herbs (optional), such as parsley or chives

**Preparation time**: 10 minutes
**Cooking time**: 15 minutes

**Directions:**
1. Preheat the Oven: Preheat your oven to 375°F (190°C).
2. Cook Onions: In an ovenproof skillet, heat the olive oil over medium heat. Add the chopped onions and sauté until translucent, about 3-4 minutes.
3. Add Broccoli: Add the steamed broccoli florets to the skillet and cook for another 2 minutes, stirring occasionally.
4. Prepare the Egg Mixture: In a bowl, whisk the eggs until well beaten. Season with salt and pepper.
5. Combine and Cook: Pour the egg mixture over the vegetables in the skillet, stirring gently to combine. Cook on the stove for 2 minutes until the edges start to set.
6. Bake the Frittata: Transfer the skillet to the preheated oven and bake for 10 minutes, or until the eggs are fully set and the top is lightly golden.
7. Serve: Slice the frittata and serve hot, garnished with fresh herbs if desired.

**Nutritional value per serving:**
- Calories: 150- Carbs: 6g- Fiber: 2g- Sugars: 2g- Protein: 12g- Saturated Fat: 2g- Unsaturated Fat: 4g

**Difficulty rating**: ★★☆☆☆

## 37. Grilled Turkey Patty

**Introduction:**
A Grilled Turkey Patty is a simple yet flavorful dish that makes for a perfect quick lunch. It's a healthier alternative to traditional beef patties, offering lean protein and a delicious taste. Paired with grilled zucchini, this meal is both satisfying and nutritious, fitting seamlessly into a balanced diet.

**Ingredients for 1 serving:**
- 4 oz ground turkey breast
- 1/4 teaspoon garlic powder
- 1/4 teaspoon onion powder
- 1/4 teaspoon salt
- 1/4 teaspoon black pepper
- 1 medium zucchini, sliced into rounds
- Olive oil spray

**Preparation time**: 10 minutes
**Cooking time**: 15 minutes

**Directions:**
1. Preheat Grill: Heat the grill to medium-high heat.
2. Season the Turkey: In a bowl, mix the ground turkey with garlic powder, onion powder, salt, and black pepper. Form the mixture into a patty.
3. Grill the Patty: Place the turkey patty on the grill. Cook for about 5-6 minutes on each side or until fully cooked and the internal temperature reaches 165°F.
4. Grill the Zucchini: While the turkey is cooking, spray the zucchini slices with olive oil and season with a pinch of salt and pepper. Grill the zucchini slices for about 2-3 minutes on each side until tender and lightly charred.

5. Serve: Serve the grilled turkey patty alongside the grilled zucchini slices.

**Nutritional value per serving:**
- Calories: 180- Carbs: 6g- Fiber: 2g- Sugars: 3g- Protein: 26g- Saturated Fat: 1g- Unsaturated Fat: 3g

**Difficulty rating**: ★★☆☆☆

# 38. Mixed Berry Salad

**Introduction:**
This Mixed Berry Salad is a refreshing and vibrant lunch option that combines the natural sweetness of berries with the creamy richness of plain nonfat yogurt. It's a perfect light meal for a busy day, providing a burst of flavor and a healthy dose of antioxidants.

**Ingredients for 1 serving:**
- 1/2 cup strawberries, sliced
- 1/2 cup blueberries
- 1/2 cup raspberries
- 1/2 cup plain nonfat Greek yogurt
- Fresh mint leaves (optional), for garnish

**Preparation time**: 5 minutes
**Cooking time**: None

**Directions:**
1. Prepare the Berries: Wash and prepare the strawberries, blueberries, and raspberries. If strawberries are large, slice them into halves or quarters.
2. Assemble the Salad: In a serving bowl, combine the berries.
3. Add Yogurt: Top the berry mixture with a dollop of plain nonfat Greek yogurt.
4. Garnish: Garnish with fresh mint leaves if desired.
5. Serve: Serve immediately, enjoying the combination of sweet and tangy flavors.

**Nutritional value per serving:**
- Calories: 120- Carbs: 23g- Fiber: 6g- Sugars: 14g- Protein: 7g- Saturated Fat: 0g- Unsaturated Fat: 0g

**Difficulty rating**: ★☆☆☆☆

# 39. Lemon Garlic Shrimp

**Introduction:**
Lemon Garlic Shrimp is a light yet flavorful dish perfect for a quick and satisfying lunch. This recipe combines the zesty freshness of lemon with the robust flavor of garlic, creating a delightful meal that's both nutritious and delicious. Served over a bed of arugula, it offers a refreshing contrast that enhances the shrimp's delicate taste.

**Ingredients for 1 serving:**
- 4 oz shrimp, peeled and deveined
- 1 clove garlic, minced
- 1 tablespoon lemon juice
- 1 teaspoon olive oil
- 1 cup arugula

- Salt and pepper, to taste
- Lemon zest (optional), for garnish

**Preparation time**: 10 minutes
**Cooking time**: 5 minutes

**Directions:**
1. Heat the Pan: Heat olive oil in a skillet over medium heat.
2. Cook the Garlic: Add the minced garlic and sauté for about 1 minute until fragrant.
3. Cook the Shrimp: Add the shrimp to the pan. Cook for 2-3 minutes on each side until the shrimp are pink and opaque.
4. Add Lemon Juice: Pour in the lemon juice, stirring to coat the shrimp evenly. Cook for an additional minute.
5. Season and Serve: Season with salt and pepper to taste. Serve the shrimp over a bed of fresh arugula. Garnish with lemon zest if desired.

**Nutritional value per serving:**
- Calories: 150- Carbs: 3g- Fiber: 1g- Sugars: 0g- Protein: 25g- Saturated Fat: 0.5g- Unsaturated Fat: 1.5g

**Difficulty rating**: ★☆☆☆☆

## 39. Spiced Lentil Stew

**Introduction:**
This Spiced Lentil Stew is a hearty and warming dish perfect for a cozy lunch. Rich in flavor and packed with nutrients, it combines lentils with aromatic spices like turmeric and cumin, along with the tanginess of tomatoes. It's a versatile dish that can be enjoyed on its own or paired with a side of fresh greens.

**Ingredients for 1 serving:**
- 1/2 cup dry lentils, rinsed
- 1/2 cup diced tomatoes
- 1/4 onion, finely chopped
- 1 clove garlic, minced
- 1 teaspoon ground turmeric
- 1 teaspoon ground cumin
- 1 teaspoon olive oil
- 2 cups vegetable broth
- Salt and pepper, to taste
- Fresh cilantro (optional), for garnish

**Preparation time**: 10 minutes
**Cooking time**: 30 minutes

**Directions:**
1. Sauté the Aromatics: In a pot, heat olive oil over medium heat. Add the onion and garlic, sautéing until softened.
2. Add Spices and Tomatoes: Stir in the turmeric and cumin, then add the diced tomatoes. Cook for about 2 minutes.
3. Cook the Lentils: Add the lentils and vegetable broth to the pot. Bring to a boil, then reduce the heat and simmer for 25-30 minutes, or until the lentils are tender.
4. Season and Serve: Season with salt and pepper to taste. Garnish with fresh cilantro if desired.

**Nutritional value per serving:**
- Calories: 220- Carbs: 35g- Fiber: 15g- Sugars: 4g- Protein: 12g- Saturated Fat: 0.5g- Unsaturated Fat: 2g

**Difficulty rating:** ★★☆☆☆

## 40. Chicken Vegetable Stir-Fry

**Introduction:**
This Chicken Vegetable Stir-Fry is a delightful, quick, and healthy meal that combines the lean protein of chicken breast with the fresh, crisp flavors of a variety of vegetables. The dish is perfect for a nutritious lunch that is both satisfying and light, making it ideal for those busy days when time is of the essence.

**Ingredients for 1 serving:**
- 4 oz chicken breast, thinly sliced
- 1/2 cup bell peppers, sliced
- 1/2 cup snap peas
- 1/4 onion, sliced
- 1 clove garlic, minced
- 1 teaspoon olive oil
- 2 tablespoons low-sodium soy sauce
- 1 teaspoon fresh ginger, grated
- Salt and pepper, to taste

**Preparation time**: 10 minutes
**Cooking time**: 10 minutes

**Directions**:
1. Prepare the Ingredients: Slice the chicken breast and vegetables, and mince the garlic and ginger.
2. Heat the Pan: In a large skillet or wok, heat olive oil over medium-high heat.
3. Cook the Chicken: Add the chicken slices and cook for 3-4 minutes until they begin to brown.
4. Add Vegetables: Add the bell peppers, snap peas, and onion. Stir-fry for another 3 minutes.
5. Flavor the Dish: Add garlic, ginger, and soy sauce to the pan, stirring to combine. Cook for an additional 2 minutes.
6. Season and Serve: Season with salt and pepper to taste, and serve hot.

**Nutritional value per serving**:
- Calories: 210- Carbs: 10g- Fiber: 3g- Sugars: 4g- Protein: 28g- Saturated Fat: 0.5g- Unsaturated Fat: 2g

**Difficulty rating**: ★☆☆☆☆

## 41. Egg White Scramble

**Introduction:**
This Egg White Scramble is a light and protein-rich option for a quick home lunch. Packed with fresh vegetables like spinach, tomatoes, and mushrooms, it offers a burst of flavor and nutrition. This dish is perfect for those looking for a low-calorie, satisfying meal that is easy to prepare.

**Ingredients for 1 serving:**
- 4 egg whites
- 1/2 cup spinach leaves, chopped
- 1/4 cup tomatoes, diced
- 1/4 cup mushrooms, sliced
- 1 clove garlic, minced
- 1 teaspoon olive oil
- Salt and pepper, to taste
- Fresh herbs (optional), for garnish

**Preparation time**: 5 minutes
**Cooking time**: 5 minutes

**Directions:**
1. Prepare the Ingredients: Chop the spinach, tomatoes, and mushrooms; mince the garlic.
2. Cook the Vegetables: In a non-stick skillet, heat olive oil over medium heat. Add the garlic and cook until fragrant, about 1 minute.
3. Add Vegetables: Add the mushrooms and tomatoes, cooking for 2 minutes until they start to soften. Add the spinach and cook until wilted.
4. Cook the Eggs: Pour in the egg whites and stir gently to scramble. Cook until the eggs are set, about 2-3 minutes.
5. Season and Serve: Season with salt and pepper. Garnish with fresh herbs if desired.

**Nutritional value per serving:**
- Calories: 120- Carbs: 5g- Fiber: 2g- Sugars: 3g- Protein: 20g- Saturated Fat: 0.5g- Unsaturated Fat: 1.5g

**Difficulty rating**: ★☆☆☆☆

## 42. Smoked Salmon Plate

**Introduction:**
The Smoked Salmon Plate is an elegant and nutritious option for lunch, perfect for those who appreciate the rich flavors of smoked fish. Paired with fresh cucumbers and tomatoes, this dish provides a balanced combination of protein and fresh vegetables, making it an ideal choice for a light and satisfying meal.

**Ingredients for 1 serving:**
- 4 oz smoked salmon, thinly sliced
- 1/2 cup cucumber, thinly sliced
- 1/2 cup tomatoes, sliced
- 1 lemon wedge
- Fresh dill (optional), for garnish

**Preparation time**: 5 minutes
**Cooking time**: None

**Directions**:
1. Prepare the Vegetables: Thinly slice the cucumber and tomatoes.
2. Arrange the Plate: Lay the smoked salmon slices on a plate. Arrange the cucumber and tomato slices alongside the salmon.

3. Garnish and Serve: Garnish with a wedge of lemon and fresh dill if desired. Squeeze the lemon over the salmon and vegetables before serving for added flavor.

**Nutritional value per serving:**
- Calories: 150- Carbs: 6g- Fiber: 2g- Sugars: 3g- Protein: 18g- Saturated Fat: 1g- Unsaturated Fat: 3g

**Difficulty rating:** ★☆☆☆☆

# 43. Herbed Yogurt Dip with Veggies

**Introduction:**
Herbed Yogurt Dip with Veggies is a refreshing and healthy lunch option, perfect for dipping fresh carrot and celery sticks. The dip is made with plain nonfat Greek yogurt and a blend of herbs, offering a creamy and flavorful accompaniment to crunchy vegetables.

**Ingredients for 1 serving:**
- 1/2 cup plain nonfat Greek yogurt
- 1 teaspoon fresh dill, chopped
- 1 teaspoon fresh parsley, chopped
- 1 teaspoon fresh chives, chopped
- 1 clove garlic, minced
- Salt and pepper, to taste
- 1 cup carrot sticks
- 1 cup celery sticks

**Preparation time:** 10 minutes
**Cooking time:** None

**Directions:**
1. Prepare the Dip: In a small bowl, combine the Greek yogurt, dill, parsley, chives, and minced garlic. Stir well to blend the flavors.
2. Season: Add salt and pepper to taste, mixing thoroughly.
3. Prepare the Vegetables: Wash and cut the carrots and celery into sticks.
4. Serve: Serve the herbed yogurt dip alongside the carrot and celery sticks. Enjoy as a refreshing and nutritious snack or light lunch.

**Nutritional value per serving:**
- Calories: 90- Carbs: 10g- Fiber: 3g- Sugars: 6g- Protein: 10g- Saturated Fat: 0g- Unsaturated Fat: 0g

**Difficulty rating:** ★☆☆☆☆

## *6.3 Salads, Soups, and More*

# 44. Cucumber Tomato Salad

**Introduction:**
This Cucumber Tomato Salad is a refreshing and simple dish that combines the crispness of cucumbers with the juicy sweetness of tomatoes. Tossed with a light lemon dressing and fresh herbs, this salad is perfect as a light lunch or a side dish.

**Ingredients for 1 serving:**
- 1 cup cucumber, chopped
- 1 cup tomatoes, chopped
- 1 tablespoon fresh lemon juice
- 1 tablespoon fresh parsley, chopped
- 1 tablespoon fresh mint, chopped (optional)
- Salt and pepper, to taste

**Preparation time**: 10 minutes
**Cooking time**: None

**Directions:**
1. Prepare the Vegetables: Chop the cucumber and tomatoes into bite-sized pieces.
2. Make the Dressing: In a bowl, whisk together the lemon juice, parsley, and mint.
3. Toss the Salad: Add the chopped cucumber and tomatoes to the bowl. Toss well to combine and coat the vegetables with the dressing.
4. Season and Serve: Season with salt and pepper to taste. Serve immediately, or chill for 15 minutes to let the flavors meld.

**Nutritional value per serving**:
- Calories: 50- Carbs: 10g- Fiber: 2g- Sugars: 5g- Protein: 1g- Saturated Fat: 0g- Unsaturated Fat: 0g

**Difficulty rating**: ★☆☆☆☆

# 45. Spicy Pumpkin Soup

**Introduction:**
This Spicy Pumpkin Soup is a warm and comforting dish, perfect for cooler days. The combination of pumpkin, onions, garlic, and a hint of chili creates a rich and flavorful soup that is both nourishing and satisfying. It's a delightful way to enjoy the natural sweetness of pumpkin with a spicy kick.

**Ingredients for 1 serving:**
- 1 cup pumpkin puree (unsweetened)
- 1/4 onion, chopped
- 1 clove garlic, minced
- 1/2 teaspoon chili powder (adjust to taste)
- 1/2 teaspoon ground cumin
- 1 cup vegetable broth (low sodium)
- 1 teaspoon olive oil
- Salt and pepper, to taste

- Fresh cilantro (optional), for garnish

**Preparation time**: 10 minutes
**Cooking time**: 20 minutes

**Directions**:
1. Sauté the Aromatics: In a saucepan, heat olive oil over medium heat. Add the chopped onion and minced garlic, sautéing until softened, about 5 minutes.
2. Add Spices and Pumpkin: Stir in the chili powder and cumin, then add the pumpkin puree. Mix well to combine.
3. Add Broth and Simmer: Pour in the vegetable broth, stirring to incorporate. Bring to a boil, then reduce the heat and simmer for 15 minutes, allowing the flavors to meld.
4. Blend the Soup: Use an immersion blender to puree the soup until smooth. If you prefer a chunkier texture, blend only a portion of the soup.
5. Season and Serve: Season with salt and pepper to taste. Garnish with fresh cilantro if desired, and serve hot.

**Nutritional value per serving:**
- Calories: 120- Carbs: 18g- Fiber: 4g- Sugars: 8g- Protein: 2g- Saturated Fat: 0g- Unsaturated Fat: 2g

**Difficulty rating**: ★★☆☆☆

## 46. Asian Chicken Salad

**Introduction:**
This Asian Chicken Salad is a vibrant and flavorful dish that combines tender shredded chicken with crisp vegetables and a tangy soy sauce dressing. It's perfect for a light yet filling lunch, offering a refreshing blend of textures and flavors that are both satisfying and nutritious.

**Ingredients for 1 serving:**
- 4 oz cooked chicken breast, shredded
- 1 cup shredded cabbage (red or green)
- 1/2 cup shredded carrots
- 1/4 cup sliced bell peppers
- 1 tablespoon fresh cilantro, chopped (optional)
- 1 tablespoon low-sodium soy sauce
- 1 teaspoon rice vinegar
- 1/2 teaspoon sesame oil
- 1/2 teaspoon honey (optional)
- 1 teaspoon sesame seeds (optional), for garnish

**Preparation time**: 15 minutes
**Cooking time**: None (using pre-cooked chicken)

**Directions:**
1. Prepare the Vegetables: Shred the cabbage, carrots, and slice the bell peppers.
2. Mix the Dressing: In a small bowl, whisk together the soy sauce, rice vinegar, sesame oil, and honey until well combined.
3. Combine Ingredients: In a large bowl, combine the shredded chicken, cabbage, carrots, bell peppers, and cilantro.
4. Toss the Salad: Pour the dressing over the salad ingredients and toss until everything is evenly coated.
5. Serve: Garnish with sesame seeds if desired. Serve immediately or chill for a refreshing cold salad.

**Nutritional value per serving:**
- Calories: 220- Carbs: 12g- Fiber: 4g- Sugars: 6g- Protein: 28g- Saturated Fat: 0.5g- Unsaturated Fat: 2g

**Difficulty rating:** ★☆☆☆☆

## 47. Beet and Orange Salad

**Introduction:**
Beet and Orange Salad is a visually stunning and deliciously refreshing dish. The earthy sweetness of roasted beets pairs beautifully with the bright, citrusy notes of fresh orange segments. Garnished with fresh mint, this salad offers a delightful combination of flavors and colors.

**Ingredients for 1 serving:**
- 1 medium beet, roasted and sliced
- 1 orange, segmented
- 1 tablespoon fresh mint leaves, chopped
- 1 tablespoon balsamic vinegar
- 1 teaspoon olive oil
- Salt and pepper, to taste

**Preparation time:** 10 minutes
**Cooking time:** 45 minutes (for roasting beets)

**Directions:**
1. Roast the Beets: Preheat the oven to 400°F (200°C). Wrap the beet in aluminum foil and roast for 45 minutes or until tender. Let cool, then peel and slice.
2. Prepare the Orange: While the beet is roasting, segment the orange, removing any seeds and pith.
3. Assemble the Salad: Arrange the beet slices and orange segments on a plate.
4. Make the Dressing: In a small bowl, whisk together the balsamic vinegar, olive oil, salt, and pepper.
5. Dress and Serve: Drizzle the dressing over the salad and garnish with fresh mint leaves. Serve immediately.

**Nutritional value per serving:**
- Calories: 120- Carbs: 24g- Fiber: 6g- Sugars: 18g- Protein: 2g- Saturated Fat: 0g- Unsaturated Fat: 2g

**Difficulty rating:** ★★☆☆☆

## 48. Vegetable Lentil Soup

**Introduction:**
Vegetable Lentil Soup is a hearty and nourishing dish perfect for a satisfying lunch. Combining the earthy flavor of lentils with a variety of fresh vegetables, this soup is rich in nutrients and offers a comforting warmth, ideal for any day.

**Ingredients for 1 serving:**
- 1/2 cup dry lentils, rinsed

- 1/2 cup carrots, diced
- 1/2 cup zucchini, diced
- 1/4 onion, chopped
- 1 clove garlic, minced
- 2 cups vegetable broth (low sodium)
- 1 teaspoon olive oil
- 1/2 teaspoon dried thyme
- 1/2 teaspoon cumin
- Salt and pepper, to taste

**Preparation time**: 10 minutes
**Cooking time**: 30 minutes

**Directions:**
1. Prepare the Vegetables: Dice the carrots and zucchini, chop the onion, and mince the garlic.
2. Sauté the Aromatics: In a large pot, heat the olive oil over medium heat. Add the onion and garlic, sautéing until translucent, about 5 minutes.
3. Add Vegetables and Lentils: Stir in the carrots, zucchini, and lentils. Add the thyme and cumin, stirring to combine.
4. Simmer the Soup: Pour in the vegetable broth and bring to a boil. Reduce the heat and simmer for 25-30 minutes, or until the lentils and vegetables are tender.
5. Season and Serve: Season with salt and pepper to taste. Serve hot, garnished with fresh herbs if desired.

**Nutritional value per serving:**
- Calories: 200- Carbs: 34g- Fiber: 12g- Sugars: 6g- Protein: 12g- Saturated Fat: 0g- Unsaturated Fat: 2g

**Difficulty rating**: ★★☆☆☆

# 49. Tuna and Egg Salad

**Introduction:**
This Tuna and Egg Salad is a protein-packed, satisfying option for a quick and healthy lunch. The combination of flaked tuna and hard-boiled eggs, mixed with crunchy onions and creamy nonfat yogurt, creates a balanced and nutritious dish.

**Ingredients for 1 serving:**
- 1 can (4 oz) tuna in water, drained
- 1 hard-boiled egg, chopped
- 1/4 cup plain nonfat Greek yogurt
- 1/4 cup onion, finely chopped
- 1 tablespoon fresh parsley, chopped
- Salt and pepper, to taste
- Lemon wedge (optional), for garnish

**Preparation time**: 10 minutes
**Cooking time**: None (using pre-cooked eggs)

**Directions:**
1. Prepare the Ingredients: Drain the tuna and chop the hard-boiled egg and onion.
2. Mix the Salad: In a bowl, combine the tuna, chopped egg, onion, and Greek yogurt. Stir well to blend.

3. Season: Add the parsley, salt, and pepper, mixing thoroughly.
4. Serve: Serve immediately, garnished with a lemon wedge for a burst of freshness.

**Nutritional value per serving:**
- Calories: 160- Carbs: 5g- Fiber: 1g- Sugars: 3g- Protein: 28g- Saturated Fat: 1g- Unsaturated Fat: 1g

**Difficulty rating:** ★☆☆☆☆

# 50. Kale and Apple Salad

**Introduction:**
Kale and Apple Salad is a delightful blend of flavors and textures, combining the hearty, nutrient-rich properties of kale with the crisp sweetness of apples. This salad is elevated with a simple vinegar dressing and a sprinkle of cinnamon, offering a refreshing and wholesome lunch option.

**Ingredients for 1 serving:**
- 2 cups kale leaves, chopped
- 1 medium apple, sliced thinly
- 1 tablespoon apple cider vinegar
- 1 teaspoon olive oil
- 1/2 teaspoon cinnamon
- Salt and pepper, to taste

**Preparation time**: 10 minutes
**Cooking time**: None

**Directions:**
1. Prepare the Kale: Wash and chop the kale leaves, removing the tough stems.
2. Slice the Apple: Thinly slice the apple, leaving the skin on for added fiber and nutrients.
3. Make the Dressing: In a small bowl, whisk together the apple cider vinegar, olive oil, salt, and pepper.
4. Assemble the Salad: In a large bowl, combine the kale and apple slices. Pour the dressing over the salad and toss well to coat.
5. Finish with Cinnamon: Sprinkle cinnamon over the salad and mix gently. Serve immediately.

**Nutritional value per serving:**
- Calories: 120- Carbs: 22g- Fiber: 6g- Sugars: 14g- Protein: 2g- Saturated Fat: 0g- Unsaturated Fat: 2g

**Difficulty rating:** ★☆☆☆☆

# 51. Spicy Black Bean Soup

**Introduction:**
This Spicy Black Bean Soup is a robust and flavorful dish, perfect for warming up on cooler days. The beans are simmered with onions, garlic, and chili, then pureed to create a smooth and satisfying soup that is both hearty and nutritious.

**Ingredients for 1 serving:**
- 1 cup black beans, cooked
- 1/4 onion, chopped
- 1 clove garlic, minced
- 1 teaspoon chili powder

- 1/2 teaspoon ground cumin
- 2 cups vegetable broth (low sodium)
- 1 teaspoon olive oil
- Salt and pepper, to taste
- Fresh cilantro (optional), for garnish

**Preparation time**: 10 minutes
**Cooking time**: 20 minutes

**Directions:**
1. Sauté the Aromatics: In a large pot, heat olive oil over medium heat. Add the chopped onion and minced garlic, sautéing until softened, about 5 minutes.
2. Add Beans and Spices: Stir in the chili powder and cumin, then add the cooked black beans.
3. Simmer: Pour in the vegetable broth, bring to a boil, then reduce heat and simmer for 15 minutes.
4. Blend the Soup: Use an immersion blender to puree the soup until smooth. For a chunkier texture, blend only a portion of the soup.
5. Season and Serve: Season with salt and pepper to taste. Garnish with fresh cilantro if desired. Serve hot.

**Nutritional value per serving**:
- Calories: 180- Carbs: 32g- Fiber: 12g- Sugars: 2g- Protein: 12g- Saturated Fat: 0g- Unsaturated Fat: 2g

**Difficulty rating**: ★★☆☆☆

## 52. Greek Salad

**Introduction:**
Greek Salad is a classic, vibrant dish that brings together fresh cucumbers, tomatoes, and onions with a simple vinegar dressing. Topped with oregano, this salad captures the essence of Mediterranean flavors in a light and refreshing meal.

**Ingredients for 1 serving:**
- 1 cup cucumber, chopped
- 1 cup tomatoes, chopped
- 1/4 cup red onion, thinly sliced
- 1 tablespoon red wine vinegar
- 1 teaspoon olive oil
- 1 teaspoon dried oregano
- Salt and pepper, to taste
- Fresh parsley (optional), for garnish

**Preparation time**: 10 minutes
**Cooking time**: None

**Directions:**
1. Prepare the Vegetables: Chop the cucumbers and tomatoes, and thinly slice the red onion.
2. Make the Dressing: In a small bowl, whisk together the red wine vinegar, olive oil, salt, and pepper.
3. Assemble the Salad: In a large bowl, combine the cucumbers, tomatoes, and red onion.
4. Dress and Toss: Pour the dressing over the salad and toss well to coat the vegetables evenly.
5. Finish with Oregano: Sprinkle dried oregano over the top. Garnish with fresh parsley if desired and serve immediately.

**Nutritional value per serving:**
- Calories: 80- Carbs: 13g- Fiber: 3g- Sugars: 6g- Protein: 2g- Saturated Fat: 0g- Unsaturated Fat: 2g

**Difficulty rating**: ★☆☆☆☆

# 53. Butternut Squash Soup

**Introduction:**
Butternut Squash Soup is a warm and comforting dish, perfect for a cozy lunch. The naturally sweet flavor of roasted butternut squash is enhanced with a touch of cinnamon and nutmeg, creating a smooth and creamy soup that is both delicious and nutritious.

**Ingredients for 1 serving:**
- 1 cup butternut squash, cubed
- 1/4 onion, chopped
- 1 clove garlic, minced
- 1/2 teaspoon olive oil
- 1 cup vegetable broth (low sodium)
- 1/4 teaspoon ground cinnamon
- 1/4 teaspoon ground nutmeg
- Salt and pepper, to taste

**Preparation time**: 10 minutes
**Cooking time**: 25 minutes (including roasting time)

**Directions:**
1. Roast the Squash: Preheat the oven to 400°F (200°C). Toss the cubed butternut squash with olive oil, salt, and pepper. Spread on a baking sheet and roast for 20 minutes or until tender.
2. Sauté the Onion and Garlic: In a pot, sauté the chopped onion and minced garlic in a little olive oil over medium heat until translucent, about 5 minutes.
3. Add Squash and Spices: Add the roasted squash, cinnamon, and nutmeg to the pot. Stir to combine.
4. Add Broth and Simmer: Pour in the vegetable broth and bring to a simmer. Cook for 5 minutes to let the flavors meld.
5. Blend the Soup: Use an immersion blender to puree the soup until smooth. For a chunkier texture, blend only a portion of the soup.
6. Season and Serve: Season with additional salt and pepper if needed. Serve hot, garnished with a sprinkle of cinnamon if desired.

**Nutritional value per serving:**
- Calories: 130- Carbs: 25g- Fiber: 5g- Sugars: 8g- Protein: 2g- Saturated Fat: 0g- Unsaturated Fat: 2g

**Difficulty rating**: ★★☆☆☆

# CHAPTER 7

# DELECTABLE DINNERS

## *7.1 FAMILY-FRIENDLY DISHES*

## 54. Grilled Chicken Skewers

**Introduction:**
Grilled Chicken Skewers are a fantastic, family-friendly dinner option that combines tender marinated chicken with colorful bell peppers and onions. This dish is perfect for a casual dinner, offering a burst of flavor and a delightful presentation.

**Ingredients for 1 serving:**
- 4 oz chicken breast, cut into cubes
- 1/2 bell pepper, cut into chunks
- 1/4 onion, cut into chunks
- 1 tablespoon olive oil
- 1 tablespoon lemon juice
- 1 teaspoon dried oregano
- 1 clove garlic, minced
- Salt and pepper, to taste
- Skewers (wooden or metal)

**Preparation time**: 15 minutes
**Cooking time:** 10 minutes

**Directions:**
1. Marinate the Chicken: In a bowl, combine olive oil, lemon juice, oregano, minced garlic, salt, and pepper. Add the chicken cubes and toss to coat. Marinate for at least 15 minutes.
2. Prepare the Vegetables: Cut the bell pepper and onion into chunks.
3. Assemble the Skewers: Thread the chicken, bell pepper, and onion pieces alternately onto skewers.
4. Grill the Skewers: Preheat the grill to medium-high heat. Grill the skewers for 5 minutes on each side, or until the chicken is cooked through and has a nice char.
5. Serve: Serve hot, garnished with fresh herbs if desired.

**Nutritional value per serving:**
- Calories: 220- Carbs: 8g- Fiber: 2g- Sugars: 4g- Protein: 26g- Saturated Fat: 1g- Unsaturated Fat: 3g

**Difficulty rating**: ★★☆☆☆

# 55. Turkey Taco Lettuce Wraps

**Introduction:**
Turkey Taco Lettuce Wraps are a light and flavorful alternative to traditional tacos, using crisp lettuce leaves as a wrap instead of tortillas. This dish is perfect for a family dinner, offering a healthy and satisfying meal with a bit of a kick.

**Ingredients for 1 serving:**
- 4 oz ground turkey breast
- 1/4 cup onion, diced
- 1/2 cup tomatoes, diced
- 1 teaspoon olive oil
- 1 teaspoon taco seasoning (low sodium)
- 1/4 cup water
- 2-3 large lettuce leaves (Romaine or Bibb lettuce)
- Fresh cilantro, chopped (optional)
- Lime wedges (optional)

**Preparation time**: 10 minutes
**Cooking time**: 10 minutes

**Directions:**
1. Cook the Turkey: In a skillet, heat olive oil over medium heat. Add the diced onion and sauté until translucent, about 3 minutes.
2. Add the Turkey and Seasoning: Add the ground turkey to the skillet and cook until browned, breaking it up with a spatula. Add the taco seasoning and water, stir well, and simmer for another 2-3 minutes.
3. Prepare the Lettuce Wraps: Wash and pat dry the lettuce leaves.
4. Assemble the Wraps: Spoon the turkey mixture into the lettuce leaves. Top with diced tomatoes and fresh cilantro.
5. Serve: Serve with lime wedges on the side for an extra burst of flavor.

**Nutritional value per serving:**
- Calories: 180- Carbs: 6g- Fiber: 2g- Sugars: 3g- Protein: 24g- Saturated Fat: 1g- Unsaturated Fat: 3g

**Difficulty rating**: ★☆☆☆☆

# 56. Vegetable Stir-Fry

**Introduction:**
This Vegetable Stir-Fry is a vibrant and healthy dinner option, featuring a mix of fresh, zero-point vegetables stir-fried with aromatic garlic and ginger. It's a quick and easy dish that's perfect for busy weeknights, offering a delightful balance of flavors and textures.

**Ingredients for 1 serving:**
- 1/2 cup snap peas
- 1/2 cup carrots, julienned
- 1/2 cup broccoli florets
- 1/4 onion, thinly sliced
- 1 clove garlic, minced
- 1 teaspoon fresh ginger, grated
- 1 teaspoon olive oil
- 1 tablespoon soy sauce (low sodium)

- 1 tablespoon water
- Salt and pepper, to taste

**Preparation time**: 10 minutes
**Cooking time**: 10 minutes

**Directions:**
1. Prepare the Vegetables: Wash and cut the vegetables. Julienne the carrots, and cut the broccoli into florets.
2. Heat the Pan: In a large skillet or wok, heat the olive oil over medium-high heat.
3. Stir-Fry the Aromatics: Add the garlic and ginger to the pan, stir-frying for about 1 minute until fragrant.
4. Cook the Vegetables: Add the onions, snap peas, carrots, and broccoli to the pan. Stir-fry for about 5-6 minutes, adding a tablespoon of water to help steam the vegetables.
5. Season and Serve: Add the soy sauce, and stir to combine. Season with salt and pepper to taste. Serve hot.

**Nutritional value per serving:**
- Calories: 120- Carbs: 22g- Fiber: 6g- Sugars: 8g- Protein: 5g- Saturated Fat: 0g- Unsaturated Fat: 2g

**Difficulty rating**: ★☆☆☆☆

# 57. Vegetable Omelettes

**Introduction:**
Vegetable Omelettes are a classic and versatile dinner option that is both satisfying and nutritious. This recipe features a fluffy egg omelette filled with fresh tomatoes, onions, and spinach, offering a delightful mix of flavors and a boost of essential nutrients.

**Ingredients for 1 serving:**
- 2 large eggs
- 1/4 cup tomatoes, diced
- 1/4 cup onion, diced
- 1/2 cup spinach, chopped
- 1 teaspoon olive oil
- Salt and pepper, to taste
- Fresh herbs (optional), for garnish

**Preparation time**: 5 minutes
**Cooking time**: 5 minutes

**Directions:**
1. Prepare the Vegetables: Dice the tomatoes and onions, and chop the spinach.
2. Beat the Eggs: In a bowl, beat the eggs with a pinch of salt and pepper.
3. Cook the Vegetables: In a non-stick skillet, heat the olive oil over medium heat. Add the onions and cook until translucent, about 2 minutes. Add the tomatoes and spinach, and cook until the spinach is wilted.
4. Cook the Omelette: Pour the beaten eggs into the skillet, swirling to distribute evenly. Cook for 2-3 minutes, or until the eggs are set.
5. Fold and Serve: Fold the omelette in half over the vegetable filling. Slide onto a plate, garnish with fresh herbs if desired, and serve hot.

**Nutritional value per serving:**
- Calories: 180- Carbs: 6g- Fiber: 2g- Sugars: 4g- Protein: 12g- Saturated Fat: 3g- Unsaturated Fat: 4g

**Difficulty rating:** ★★☆☆☆

# 58. Turkey Meatball Soup

**Introduction:**
Turkey Meatball Soup is a comforting and hearty dish that features tender turkey breast meatballs simmered in a flavorful vegetable broth with herbs. This soup is perfect for a family dinner, offering warmth and nourishment in every bite.

**Ingredients for 1 serving:**
- 4 oz ground turkey breast
- 1/4 cup onion, finely chopped
- 1 clove garlic, minced
- 1/4 teaspoon dried oregano
- 1/4 teaspoon dried basil
- Salt and pepper, to taste
- 1 teaspoon olive oil
- 2 cups vegetable broth (low sodium)
- 1/2 cup carrots, sliced
- 1/2 cup celery, sliced
- Fresh parsley, chopped (optional)

**Preparation time:** 15 minutes
**Cooking time:** 20 minutes

**Directions:**
1. Prepare the Meatballs: In a bowl, mix the ground turkey, chopped onion, minced garlic, oregano, basil, salt, and pepper. Form into small meatballs.
2. Sauté the Meatballs: In a large pot, heat olive oil over medium heat. Add the meatballs and cook until browned on all sides, about 5 minutes.
3. Add Vegetables and Broth: Add the carrots and celery to the pot, then pour in the vegetable broth. Bring to a boil.
4. Simmer the Soup: Reduce heat and simmer for 15 minutes, or until the meatballs are cooked through and the vegetables are tender.
5. Serve: Garnish with fresh parsley if desired. Serve hot.

**Nutritional value per serving:**
- Calories: 220- Carbs: 12g- Fiber: 3g- Sugars: 5g- Protein: 25g- Saturated Fat: 1g- Unsaturated Fat: 3g

**Difficulty rating:** ★★☆☆☆

# 59. Egg and Veggie Fried Rice

**Introduction:**
This Egg and Veggie Fried "Rice" is a low-carb twist on a classic dish, using cauliflower rice instead of traditional rice. Packed with eggs and a variety of colorful vegetables, it's a nutritious and satisfying dinner option that the whole family will love.

**Ingredients for 1 serving:**
- 1 cup cauliflower rice
- 2 large eggs
- 1/4 cup bell pepper, diced
- 1/4 cup peas
- 1/4 cup carrots, diced
- 1 clove garlic, minced
- 1 teaspoon soy sauce (low sodium)
- 1 teaspoon olive oil
- Salt and pepper, to taste
- Fresh scallions, chopped (optional)

**Preparation time**: 10 minutes
**Cooking time:** 10 minutes

**Directions:**
1. Prepare the Vegetables: Dice the bell pepper and carrots. Mince the garlic.
2. Cook the Eggs: In a large skillet, heat half of the olive oil over medium heat. Beat the eggs, pour into the skillet, and scramble until cooked through. Remove from the skillet and set aside.
3. Sauté the Vegetables: In the same skillet, heat the remaining olive oil. Add the garlic and sauté for 1 minute. Add the bell pepper, peas, and carrots, cooking until tender, about 3-4 minutes.
4. Add Cauliflower Rice: Stir in the cauliflower rice and cook for another 3-4 minutes until tender.
5. Combine and Season: Return the scrambled eggs to the skillet, add the soy sauce, and stir to combine. Season with salt and pepper to taste.
6. Serve: Garnish with chopped scallions if desired. Serve hot.

**Nutritional value per serving:**
- Calories: 180- Carbs: 12g- Fiber: 4g- Sugars: 5g- Protein: 12g- Saturated Fat: 1g- Unsaturated Fat: 3g

**Difficulty rating**: ★☆☆☆☆

## *7.2 Quick Dinners in 30 Minutes or Less*

# 60. Shrimp and Garlic Spinach

**Introduction:**
This dish combines succulent shrimp with a generous serving of spinach, all brought together with the aromatic flavors of garlic. It's a quick and delicious dinner option that is both light and satisfying, perfect for those looking to enjoy a healthy meal without spending hours in the kitchen.

**Ingredients for 1 serving:**
- 4 oz shrimp, peeled and deveined
- 2 cups spinach leaves
- 2 cloves garlic, minced
- 1 teaspoon olive oil
- 1 tablespoon lemon juice
- Salt and pepper, to taste

**Preparation time**: 5 minutes
**Cooking time**: 10 minutes

**Directions:**
1. Prepare the Ingredients: Mince the garlic and wash the spinach leaves.
2. Cook the Shrimp: In a large skillet, heat the olive oil over medium heat. Add the shrimp and garlic, cooking until the shrimp turn pink and opaque, about 2-3 minutes per side. Remove the shrimp from the skillet and set aside.
3. Sauté the Spinach: In the same skillet, add the spinach and lemon juice. Cook until the spinach is wilted, about 2-3 minutes.
4. Combine and Season: Return the shrimp to the skillet, mix with the spinach, and season with salt and pepper to taste.
5. Serve: Serve hot, garnished with extra lemon wedges if desired.

**Nutritional value per serving:**
- Calories: 180- Carbs: 4g- Fiber: 2g- Sugars: 1g- Protein: 24g- Saturated Fat: 0.5g- Unsaturated Fat: 2g

**Difficulty rating**: ★☆☆☆☆

# 61. Chicken Chili

**Introduction:**
Chicken Chili is a hearty and flavorful dish that's easy to prepare and perfect for a quick dinner. This recipe uses ground chicken breast, tomatoes, and chili spices to create a warm and comforting meal that's both nutritious and delicious.

**Ingredients for 1 serving:**
- 4 oz ground chicken breast
- 1/2 cup diced tomatoes
- 1/4 cup onion, chopped
- 1 clove garlic, minced
- 1 teaspoon chili powder

- 1/2 teaspoon ground cumin
- 1/4 teaspoon paprika
- 1/4 teaspoon salt
- 1/4 teaspoon pepper
- 1 teaspoon olive oil
- 1/4 cup water
- Fresh cilantro (optional), for garnish

**Preparation time**: 5 minutes
**Cooking time**: 20 minutes

**Directions:**
1. Prepare the Ingredients: Chop the onion and mince the garlic.
2. Cook the Chicken: In a large pot, heat the olive oil over medium heat. Add the ground chicken and cook until browned, breaking it apart with a spoon.
3. Add Aromatics: Add the onion and garlic to the pot, sautéing until softened, about 3 minutes.
4. Add Tomatoes and Spices: Stir in the diced tomatoes, chili powder, cumin, paprika, salt, and pepper.
5. Simmer: Add water to the pot, bring to a boil, then reduce heat and simmer for 15 minutes, allowing the flavors to meld.
6. Serve: Serve hot, garnished with fresh cilantro if desired.

**Nutritional value per serving:**
- Calories: 220- Carbs: 10g- Fiber: 3g- Sugars: 5g- Protein: 26g- Saturated Fat: 1g- Unsaturated Fat: 3g

**Difficulty rating**: ★★☆☆☆

## 62. Stir-Fried Turkey and Peppers

**Introduction:**
Stir-Fried Turkey and Peppers is a simple yet flavorful dish that brings together lean ground turkey and vibrant bell peppers in a savory soy sauce. This quick and easy meal is perfect for those busy evenings when you want something delicious and healthy.

**Ingredients for 1 serving:**
- 4 oz ground turkey breast
- 1/2 cup bell peppers, sliced (any color)
- 1/4 onion, sliced
- 1 clove garlic, minced
- 1 tablespoon soy sauce (low sodium)
- 1 teaspoon olive oil
- 1/4 teaspoon ground black pepper
- 1/4 teaspoon crushed red pepper flakes (optional)
- Fresh cilantro, chopped (optional)

**Preparation time**: 5 minutes
**Cooking time**: 10 minutes

**Directions**:
1. Prepare the Ingredients: Slice the bell peppers and onion, and mince the garlic.
2. Cook the Turkey: In a large skillet, heat the olive oil over medium-high heat. Add the ground turkey and cook until browned, breaking it apart with a spoon, about 5 minutes.

3. Add the Vegetables: Add the sliced bell peppers, onion, and minced garlic to the skillet. Cook for another 3-4 minutes, or until the vegetables are tender.
4. Season and Finish: Stir in the soy sauce and ground black pepper. Add crushed red pepper flakes if desired for extra heat. Cook for an additional minute, stirring well to combine the flavors.
5. Serve: Serve hot, garnished with fresh cilantro if desired.

**Nutritional value per serving:**
- Calories: 210- Carbs: 7g- Fiber: 2g- Sugars: 4g- Protein: 26g- Saturated Fat: 1g- Unsaturated Fat: 3g

**Difficulty rating**: ★☆☆☆☆

# 63. Broccoli and Chicken Stir Fry

**Introduction:**
This Broccoli and Chicken Stir Fry is a delightful combination of tender chicken breast and crisp broccoli, all brought together with a simple garlic sauce. It's a nutritious and satisfying dish that can be prepared in just minutes, making it an excellent choice for a quick dinner.

**Ingredients for 1 serving:**
- 4 oz chicken breast, thinly sliced
- 1 cup broccoli florets
- 1 clove garlic, minced
- 1 teaspoon olive oil
- 1 tablespoon soy sauce (low sodium)
- 1 tablespoon water
- 1/4 teaspoon ground black pepper
- 1/2 teaspoon cornstarch (optional, for thickening)
- Fresh lemon wedges (optional)

**Preparation time**: 5 minutes
**Cooking time**: 10 minutes

**Directions:**
1. Prepare the Ingredients: Thinly slice the chicken breast and mince the garlic. Cut the broccoli into small florets.
2. Cook the Chicken: In a large skillet or wok, heat the olive oil over medium-high heat. Add the chicken slices and cook until browned and cooked through, about 4-5 minutes. Remove from the skillet and set aside.
3. Sauté the Broccoli and Garlic: In the same skillet, add the broccoli florets and minced garlic. Stir-fry for 3 minutes, or until the broccoli is tender-crisp.
4. Add Sauce and Combine: Return the chicken to the skillet. In a small bowl, mix the soy sauce, water, ground black pepper, and cornstarch (if using). Pour the sauce over the chicken and broccoli, stirring to combine. Cook for an additional 1-2 minutes until the sauce thickens slightly.
5. Serve: Serve hot, garnished with fresh lemon wedges if desired.

**Nutritional value per serving**:
- Calories: 200- Carbs: 10g- Fiber: 4g- Sugars: 3g- Protein: 27g- Saturated Fat: 1g- Unsaturated Fat: 3g

**Difficulty rating**: ★★☆☆☆

# 64. Egg Drop Soup

**Introduction:**
Egg Drop Soup is a light and delicate dish that features a simple broth infused with the flavors of fresh spring onions and tender strands of whisked eggs. This quick and easy recipe is perfect for a comforting dinner, offering a warm and soothing experience.

**Ingredients for 1 serving:**
- 1 1/2 cups chicken broth (low sodium)
- 2 large eggs, beaten
- 1 teaspoon soy sauce (optional)
- 1/4 teaspoon ground white pepper
- 1/4 cup spring onions, chopped
- 1 teaspoon cornstarch (optional, for thickening)
- 2 tablespoons water (if using cornstarch)
- Fresh cilantro, chopped (optional)

**Preparation time**: 5 minutes
**Cooking time**: 10 minutes

**Directions:**
1. Prepare the Ingredients: Beat the eggs in a bowl. Chop the spring onions.
2. Heat the Broth: In a medium pot, bring the chicken broth to a boil over medium heat. Add the soy sauce (if using) and ground white pepper.
3. Create the Egg Ribbons: Reduce the heat to low. Slowly drizzle the beaten eggs into the hot broth while stirring gently with a fork to create thin ribbons.
4. Thicken the Soup (optional): If a thicker consistency is desired, mix the cornstarch with water to form a slurry. Stir it into the soup and cook for another 1-2 minutes until thickened.
5. Add Spring Onions: Add the chopped spring onions and cook for an additional minute.
6. Serve: Serve hot, garnished with fresh cilantro if desired.

**Nutritional value per serving:**
- Calories: 100- Carbs: 3g- Fiber: 1g- Sugars: 1g- Protein: 10g- Saturated Fat: 1g- Unsaturated Fat: 2g

**Difficulty rating**: ★☆☆☆☆

# 65. Grilled Salmon Salad

**Introduction:**
Grilled Salmon Salad is a light and nutritious dinner option that combines the rich flavors of grilled salmon with a fresh bed of greens and crisp vegetables. This dish is both satisfying and elegant, making it perfect for a quick yet impressive meal.

**Ingredients for 1 serving:**
- 4 oz salmon fillet
- 2 cups mixed salad greens (such as arugula, spinach, and romaine)
- 1/2 cup cucumber, sliced
- 1/2 cup cherry tomatoes, halved
- 1 tablespoon olive oil
- 1 tablespoon lemon juice
- Salt and pepper, to taste
- Fresh dill (optional), for garnish

**Preparation time**: 5 minutes
**Cooking time**: 10 minutes

**Directions:**

1. Prepare the Salmon: Preheat the grill or a grill pan over medium-high heat. Season the salmon fillet with salt and pepper.
2. Grill the Salmon: Brush the grill or pan with olive oil to prevent sticking. Grill the salmon for about 4-5 minutes per side, or until it flakes easily with a fork. Remove from the grill and let rest.
3. Prepare the Salad: While the salmon is grilling, arrange the mixed salad greens on a plate. Top with sliced cucumber and halved cherry tomatoes.
4. Dress the Salad: Drizzle the salad with olive oil and lemon juice. Season with salt and pepper to taste.
5. Serve: Place the grilled salmon on top of the salad. Garnish with fresh dill if desired. Serve immediately.

**Nutritional value per serving:**

- Calories: 300- Carbs: 10g- Fiber: 4g- Sugars: 4g- Protein: 27g- Saturated Fat: 2g- Unsaturated Fat: 10g

**Difficulty rating**: ★★☆☆☆

## 7.3 Special Occasion Recipes

# 66. Seafood Paella with Cauliflower Rice

**Introduction:**
This lighter version of the classic Spanish dish uses cauliflower rice to keep the meal low in calories while still offering the rich flavors of saffron, shrimp, and scallops. It's perfect for a special occasion when you want to impress without straying from your dietary goals.

**Ingredients for 1 serving:**
- 2 oz shrimp, peeled and deveined
- 2 oz scallops
- 1 cup cauliflower rice
- 1/2 cup bell peppers, diced
- 1/4 cup green peas
- 1/4 cup onion, chopped
- 1 clove garlic, minced
- 1/2 teaspoon saffron threads
- 1/2 cup chicken broth (low sodium)
- 1 tablespoon olive oil
- Salt and pepper, to taste
- Fresh parsley, chopped (optional)

**Preparation time**: 10 minutes
**Cooking time**: 20 minutes

**Directions:**
1. Prepare the Ingredients: Dice the bell peppers and onion, and mince the garlic. Rinse the shrimp and scallops.
2. Sauté the Aromatics: In a large skillet, heat the olive oil over medium heat. Add the onion, garlic, and bell peppers, sautéing until softened, about 5 minutes.
3. Add Seafood and Saffron: Add the shrimp and scallops to the skillet, cooking for about 2 minutes until they begin to turn opaque. Sprinkle the saffron threads over the mixture.
4. Add Cauliflower Rice and Broth: Stir in the cauliflower rice, green peas, and chicken broth. Cook for another 10 minutes, or until the seafood is fully cooked and the cauliflower rice is tender.
5. Season and Serve: Season with salt and pepper to taste. Garnish with fresh parsley if desired. Serve hot.

**Nutritional value per serving:**
- Calories: 250- Carbs: 10g- Fiber: 4g- Sugars: 4g- Protein: 25g- Saturated Fat: 1g- Unsaturated Fat: 4g

**Difficulty rating**: ★★★☆☆

# 67. Roast Turkey Breast with Herbs

**Introduction:**
A beautifully roasted turkey breast, seasoned with a blend of aromatic herbs, is an elegant and festive main course that's both healthy and delicious. This dish is ideal for special occasions, offering a tender and juicy centerpiece to your meal.

**Ingredients for 1 serving:**
- 4 oz turkey breast, boneless and skinless
- 1 tablespoon olive oil
- 1 teaspoon fresh rosemary, chopped
- 1 teaspoon fresh thyme, chopped
- 1 teaspoon fresh sage, chopped
- 1 clove garlic, minced
- Salt and pepper, to taste
- Lemon wedges (optional, for garnish)

**Preparation time**: 10 minutes
**Cooking time**: 25 minutes

**Directions:**
1. Preheat the Oven: Preheat the oven to 375°F (190°C).
2. Prepare the Herb Mixture: In a small bowl, combine the olive oil, chopped rosemary, thyme, sage, and minced garlic.
3. Season the Turkey: Rub the turkey breast with the herb mixture, coating evenly. Season with salt and pepper.
4. Roast the Turkey: Place the turkey breast on a baking sheet. Roast in the preheated oven for 25 minutes, or until the internal temperature reaches 165°F (74°C).
5. Rest and Serve: Remove from the oven and let rest for 5 minutes before slicing. Garnish with lemon wedges if desired. Serve warm.

**Nutritional value per serving:**
- Calories: 210- Carbs: 1g- Fiber: 0g- Sugars: 0g- Protein: 32g- Saturated Fat: 1g- Unsaturated Fat: 5g

**Difficulty rating**: ★★☆☆☆

# 68. Grilled Lemon-Herb Fish

**Introduction:**
This Grilled Lemon-Herb Fish is a light and refreshing dish, perfect for special occasions. The delicate flavors of the white fish are beautifully complemented by a marinade of lemon juice and fresh herbs, resulting in a dish that's both elegant and healthy.

**Ingredients for 1 serving:**
- 4 oz white fish fillet (such as cod, tilapia, or halibut)
- 2 tablespoons lemon juice
- 1 tablespoon olive oil
- 1 teaspoon fresh dill, chopped
- 1 teaspoon fresh parsley, chopped
- 1 clove garlic, minced
- Salt and pepper, to taste
- Lemon wedges (for garnish)

**Preparation time**: 10 minutes
**Cooking time**: 10 minutes

**Directions:**
1. Marinate the Fish: In a small bowl, combine the lemon juice, olive oil, dill, parsley, and minced garlic. Season the fish fillet with salt and pepper, then pour the marinade over the fish. Let it marinate for at least 10 minutes.
2. Preheat the Grill: Preheat the grill or grill pan to medium-high heat.
3. Grill the Fish: Grill the fish for about 3-4 minutes per side, or until the fish is opaque and flakes easily with a fork.
4. Serve: Serve the fish hot, garnished with lemon wedges and additional fresh herbs if desired.

**Nutritional value per serving:**
- Calories: 220- Carbs: 2g- Fiber: 1g- Sugars: 0g- Protein: 25g- Saturated Fat: 1g- Unsaturated Fat: 6g

**Difficulty rating**: ★☆☆☆☆

## 69. Chicken and Mushroom Stew

**Introduction:**
This hearty Chicken and Mushroom Stew is perfect for a cozy evening, offering rich flavors and comforting warmth. The combination of tender chicken breast and earthy mushrooms, cooked with herbs, creates a stew that's both satisfying and nutritious.

**Ingredients for 1 serving:**
- 4 oz chicken breast, cubed
- 1 cup mushrooms, sliced
- 1/4 cup onion, chopped
- 1 clove garlic, minced
- 1/2 cup chicken broth (low sodium)
- 1 tablespoon olive oil
- 1 teaspoon fresh thyme, chopped
- 1 teaspoon fresh rosemary, chopped
- Salt and pepper, to taste

**Preparation time**: 10 minutes
**Cooking time**: 25 minutes

**Directions:**
1. Prepare the Ingredients: Cube the chicken breast, slice the mushrooms, chop the onion, and mince the garlic.
2. Cook the Chicken: In a large pot, heat the olive oil over medium heat. Add the cubed chicken and cook until browned, about 5 minutes. Remove from the pot and set aside.
3. Sauté the Vegetables: In the same pot, add the onion and garlic, sautéing until softened, about 3 minutes. Add the mushrooms and cook until they release their moisture and begin to brown.
4. Simmer the Stew: Return the chicken to the pot. Add the chicken broth, thyme, and rosemary. Bring to a simmer, then reduce heat and cook for 15 minutes, or until the chicken is cooked through and the stew has thickened.
5. Season and Serve: Season with salt and pepper to taste. Serve hot, garnished with additional fresh herbs if desired.

**Nutritional value per serving:**
- Calories: 250- Carbs: 8g- Fiber: 2g- Sugars: 3g- Protein: 27g- Saturated Fat: 1g- Unsaturated Fat: 5g

**Difficulty rating:** ★★☆☆☆

# 70. Poached Salmon with Dill Sauce

**Introduction:**
This elegant Poached Salmon with Dill Sauce combines the delicate flavors of salmon with a light, creamy yogurt-dill sauce. It's a perfect dish for special occasions, offering a sophisticated yet simple meal that's both healthy and delicious.

**Ingredients for 1 serving:**
- 4 oz salmon fillet
- 1 cup water
- 1 tablespoon lemon juice
- 1 bay leaf
- 1 teaspoon whole peppercorns
- 1/4 cup plain nonfat Greek yogurt
- 1 tablespoon fresh dill, chopped
- 1 teaspoon lemon zest
- Salt and pepper, to taste

**Preparation time**: 10 minutes
**Cooking time**: 15 minutes

**Directions:**
1. Prepare the Poaching Liquid: In a large skillet, combine the water, lemon juice, bay leaf, and peppercorns. Bring to a simmer over medium heat.
2. Poach the Salmon: Gently place the salmon fillet in the simmering liquid. Cover and poach for 10 minutes, or until the salmon is opaque and flakes easily with a fork. Remove the salmon and keep warm.
3. Prepare the Dill Sauce: In a small bowl, mix the Greek yogurt, chopped dill, and lemon zest. Season with salt and pepper to taste.
4. Serve: Plate the poached salmon and top with the yogurt-dill sauce. Garnish with additional fresh dill if desired.

**Nutritional value per serving:**
- Calories: 180- Carbs: 3g- Fiber: 0g- Sugars: 2g- Protein: 23g- Saturated Fat: 1g- Unsaturated Fat: 5g

**Difficulty rating:** ★☆☆☆☆

# 71. Eggplant Rollatini

**Introduction:**
Eggplant Rollatini is a delightful Italian-inspired dish that features grilled eggplant slices filled with a savory mixture of spinach and garlic. This dish is not only flavorful but also visually appealing, making it a great choice for a special dinner.

**Ingredients for 1 serving:**
- 1 medium eggplant, sliced lengthwise into 1/4-inch slices
- 1 cup fresh spinach, chopped
- 2 cloves garlic, minced
- 1 tablespoon olive oil
- 1/4 cup plain nonfat Greek yogurt
- 1 tablespoon fresh basil, chopped
- Salt and pepper, to taste
- 1/4 cup marinara sauce (low sodium, optional)

**Preparation time**: 15 minutes
**Cooking time**: 20 minutes

**Directions:**
1. Grill the Eggplant: Preheat a grill or grill pan over medium-high heat. Brush the eggplant slices with olive oil and season with salt and pepper. Grill for 3-4 minutes per side, until tender and slightly charred. Set aside.
2. Prepare the Filling: In a skillet, heat the remaining olive oil over medium heat. Add the minced garlic and chopped spinach, cooking until the spinach is wilted. Remove from heat and mix in the Greek yogurt and fresh basil.
3. Assemble the Rollatini: Lay out the grilled eggplant slices and spoon a portion of the spinach mixture onto each slice. Roll up the eggplant slices and place them in a baking dish.
4. Bake the Rollatini: Preheat the oven to 350°F (175°C). Spoon marinara sauce over the eggplant rolls if desired. Bake for 10 minutes, or until heated through.
5. Serve: Serve hot, garnished with additional fresh basil if desired.

**Nutritional value per serving**:
- Calories: 200- Carbs: 12g- Fiber: 5g- Sugars: 7g- Protein: 5g- Saturated Fat: 1g- Unsaturated Fat: 7g

**Difficulty rating**: ★★☆☆☆

# 72. Stuffed Bell Peppers

**Introduction:**
Stuffed Bell Peppers are a vibrant and flavorful dish perfect for a special occasion. This recipe uses a savory mixture of ground chicken and spices to fill colorful bell peppers, creating a meal that is both visually appealing and deliciously satisfying.

**Ingredients for 1 serving:**
- 1 large bell pepper (any color), halved and seeds removed
- 4 oz ground chicken breast
- 1/4 cup onion, chopped
- 1 clove garlic, minced
- 1/4 cup tomatoes, diced
- 1 tablespoon fresh parsley, chopped
- 1/2 teaspoon cumin
- 1/2 teaspoon paprika
- 1/2 teaspoon oregano
- 1 tablespoon olive oil
- Salt and pepper, to taste

**Preparation time**: 15 minutes

**Cooking time**: 30 minutes

**Directions:**
1. Preheat the Oven: Preheat your oven to 375°F (190°C).
2. Prepare the Filling: In a skillet, heat the olive oil over medium heat. Add the onion and garlic, sautéing until softened. Add the ground chicken, cooking until browned and fully cooked. Stir in the diced tomatoes, parsley, cumin, paprika, oregano, salt, and pepper. Cook for an additional 5 minutes to allow flavors to meld.
3. Stuff the Peppers: Place the bell pepper halves in a baking dish. Spoon the chicken mixture into each half, filling them generously.
4. Bake: Cover the dish with aluminum foil and bake in the preheated oven for 20 minutes. Remove the foil and bake for an additional 10 minutes, or until the peppers are tender.
5. Serve: Serve the stuffed bell peppers hot, garnished with extra parsley if desired.

**Nutritional value per serving:**
- Calories: 250- Carbs: 12g- Fiber: 4g- Sugars: 6g- Protein: 28g- Saturated Fat: 2g- Unsaturated Fat: 8g

**Difficulty rating**: ★★☆☆☆

# 73. Vegetable and Shrimp Kabobs

**Introduction:**
These Vegetable and Shrimp Kabobs are a delightful and healthy option for a special dinner. The combination of fresh vegetables and succulent shrimp, marinated and grilled to perfection, offers a colorful and nutritious dish that's sure to impress.

**Ingredients for 1 serving:**
- 4 oz shrimp, peeled and deveined
- 1/2 cup bell peppers, cut into chunks
- 1/2 cup zucchini, sliced
- 1/2 cup cherry tomatoes
- 1/4 cup red onion, cut into chunks
- 2 tablespoons olive oil
- 1 tablespoon lemon juice
- 1 teaspoon dried oregano
- 1 teaspoon garlic powder
- Salt and pepper, to taste

**Preparation time**: 15 minutes
**Cooking time**: 10 minutes

**Directions:**
1. Marinate the Shrimp and Vegetables: In a large bowl, combine the olive oil, lemon juice, oregano, garlic powder, salt, and pepper. Add the shrimp and vegetables, tossing to coat. Marinate for at least 10 minutes.
2. Prepare the Kabobs: Thread the shrimp and vegetables onto skewers, alternating the ingredients.
3. Preheat the Grill: Preheat the grill or a grill pan over medium-high heat.
4. Grill the Kabobs: Grill the kabobs for 3-4 minutes per side, or until the shrimp are cooked through and the vegetables are tender and slightly charred.
5. Serve: Serve the kabobs hot, with extra lemon wedges on the side if desired.

**Nutritional value per serving:**
- Calories: 200- Carbs: 10g- Fiber: 3g- Sugars: 5g- Protein: 22g- Saturated Fat: 1g- Unsaturated Fat: 7g

**Difficulty rating**: ★☆☆☆☆

# 74. Moroccan Chicken Tagine

**Introduction:**
Moroccan Chicken Tagine is a flavorful and aromatic dish, perfect for special occasions. This dish features tender chicken breast slow-cooked with a medley of spices, tomatoes, and olives, creating a rich and satisfying meal that's sure to impress.

**Ingredients for 1 serving:**
- 4 oz chicken breast, cubed
- 1/2 cup tomatoes, diced
- 1/4 cup green olives, pitted and halved
- 1/4 cup onion, chopped
- 1 clove garlic, minced
- 1 teaspoon ground cumin
- 1 teaspoon ground coriander
- 1/2 teaspoon ground cinnamon
- 1/2 teaspoon ground turmeric
- 1 tablespoon olive oil
- 1/2 cup chicken broth (low sodium)
- Salt and pepper, to taste
- Fresh cilantro, chopped (for garnish)

**Preparation time**: 15 minutes
**Cooking time**: 45 minutes

**Directions:**
1. Prepare the Spices and Vegetables: In a small bowl, combine the cumin, coriander, cinnamon, and turmeric. Chop the onion, garlic, and tomatoes.
2. Brown the Chicken: In a tagine or heavy-bottomed pot, heat the olive oil over medium heat. Add the chicken and cook until browned on all sides. Remove the chicken and set aside.
3. Sauté the Vegetables: In the same pot, add the onion and garlic. Sauté until softened, about 5 minutes. Add the spice mixture and cook for another minute, stirring constantly.
4. Simmer the Tagine: Add the diced tomatoes, chicken broth, olives, and browned chicken to the pot. Bring to a simmer, then reduce the heat to low. Cover and cook for 30 minutes, stirring occasionally, until the chicken is tender and the flavors are well blended.
5. Season and Serve: Season with salt and pepper to taste. Serve hot, garnished with fresh cilantro.

**Nutritional value per serving**:
- Calories: 280- Carbs: 10g- Fiber: 3g- Sugars: 4g- Protein: 30g- Saturated Fat: 1g- Unsaturated Fat: 10g

**Difficulty rating**: ★★☆☆☆

# CHAPTER 8

# SNACKS AND SIDES

## *8.1 Snacks for Every Craving*

## 75. Cucumber and Dill Sticks

**Introduction:**
Cucumber and Dill Sticks are a refreshing and crisp snack that's perfect for any time of day. This simple yet flavorful dish combines the cool crunch of cucumbers with the aromatic taste of fresh dill and a hint of vinegar, making it a delightful and hydrating snack.

**Ingredients for 1 serving:**
- 1 medium cucumber, sliced into sticks
- 1 tablespoon fresh dill, chopped
- 1 tablespoon white vinegar
- Salt and pepper, to taste

**Preparation time**: 5 minutes
**Cooking time**: None

**Directions:**
1. Prepare the Cucumber: Wash the cucumber thoroughly. Slice it into sticks, about 4 inches long and 1/2 inch thick.
2. Season the Cucumber: Place the cucumber sticks in a bowl. Sprinkle the chopped dill over the cucumber.
3. Add Vinegar and Seasoning: Drizzle the white vinegar over the cucumber sticks. Season with salt and pepper to taste. Toss gently to combine.
4. Serve: Serve immediately for a fresh and crunchy snack.

**Nutritional value per serving:**
- Calories: 16- Carbs: 3g- Fiber: 1g- Sugars: 2g- Protein: 0g- Saturated Fat: 0g- Unsaturated Fat: 0g

**Difficulty rating**: ★☆☆☆☆

## 76. Grilled Zucchini Slices

**Introduction:**
Grilled Zucchini Slices are a delicious and healthy snack or side dish. The grilling process enhances the natural sweetness of the zucchini, and the salt-free herb mix adds a burst of flavor without any extra sodium.

**Ingredients for 1 serving:**
- 1 medium zucchini, sliced into rounds
- 1 tablespoon olive oil
- 1 teaspoon salt-free herb mix (such as Italian seasoning or herbes de Provence)
- Salt and pepper, to taste

**Preparation time**: 5 minutes
**Cooking time**: 8 minutes

**Directions:**
1. Preheat the Grill: Preheat your grill or grill pan to medium-high heat.
2. Prepare the Zucchini: Slice the zucchini into 1/4-inch thick rounds. Brush each slice with olive oil.
3. Season the Zucchini: Sprinkle the salt-free herb mix evenly over the zucchini slices. Season with salt and pepper to taste.
4. Grill the Zucchini: Place the zucchini slices on the grill. Grill for 3-4 minutes on each side, or until tender and grill marks appear.
5. Serve: Serve hot or at room temperature as a snack or side dish.

**Nutritional value per serving:**
- Calories: 50- Carbs: 4g- Fiber: 1g- Sugars: 2g- Protein: 1g- Saturated Fat: 1g- Unsaturated Fat: 3g

# 77. Fruit Salad

**Introduction**:
This Fruit Salad is a delightful medley of fresh, zero-point fruits, offering a natural sweetness that satisfies cravings healthily. The addition of a dash of cinnamon enhances the flavors, making this a perfect snack for any time of the day.

**Ingredients for 1 serving:**
- 1/2 cup strawberries, sliced
- 1/2 cup oranges, segmented
- 1/2 cup apples, chopped
- 1/4 teaspoon ground cinnamon

**Preparation time**: 10 minutes
**Cooking time**: None

**Directions:**
1. Prepare the Fruits: Wash and prepare the strawberries, oranges, and apples. Slice the strawberries, segment the oranges, and chop the apples into bite-sized pieces.
2. Combine the Fruits: In a mixing bowl, combine the strawberries, oranges, and apples.
3. Add Cinnamon: Sprinkle the ground cinnamon over the fruit mixture. Gently toss to combine, ensuring the cinnamon evenly coats the fruit.
4. Serve: Serve the fruit salad immediately for the freshest taste.

**Nutritional value per serving:**
- Calories: 80- Carbs: 21g- Fiber: 4g- Sugars: 16g- Protein: 1g- Saturated Fat: 0g- Unsaturated Fat: 0g

**Difficulty rating**: ★☆☆☆☆

## 78. Pickled Vegetables

**Introduction:**
Pickled Vegetables are a tangy and crunchy snack, perfect for satisfying salty cravings without the guilt. This recipe uses a simple vinegar and spice solution to pickle a variety of vegetables, creating a versatile and flavorful addition to any meal or as a stand-alone snack.

**Ingredients for 1 serving:**
- 1/2 cup carrots, julienned
- 1/2 cup green beans, trimmed
- 1/4 cup cauliflower florets
- 1/2 cup white vinegar
- 1/2 cup water
- 1 tablespoon salt
- 1 teaspoon sugar
- 1 teaspoon mustard seeds
- 1 teaspoon black peppercorns
- 1 garlic clove, sliced
- 1 bay leaf

**Preparation time:** 15 minutes
**Cooking time**: 10 minutes

**Directions:**
1. Prepare the Vegetables: Wash and prepare the vegetables. Julien the carrots, trim the green beans, and break the cauliflower into small florets.
2. Make the Pickling Brine: In a small saucepan, combine the white vinegar, water, salt, sugar, mustard seeds, black peppercorns, garlic, and bay leaf. Bring to a boil over medium heat, then reduce to a simmer.
3. Blanch the Vegetables: In a separate pot, blanch the vegetables in boiling water for 1-2 minutes, then immediately transfer them to an ice bath to stop the cooking process.
4. Pickle the Vegetables: Drain the vegetables and place them in a jar. Pour the hot pickling brine over the vegetables, ensuring they are fully submerged. Let cool to room temperature, then seal the jar and refrigerate for at least 1 hour before serving.
5. Serve: Serve the pickled vegetables chilled as a snack or side dish.

**Nutritional value per serving:**
- Calories: 35- Carbs: 7g- Fiber: 2g- Sugars: 2g- Protein: 1g- Saturated Fat: 0g- Unsaturated Fat: 0g

**Difficulty rating**: ★★☆☆☆

## 79. Chicken and Celery Bites

**Introduction:**
Chicken and Celery Bites offer a satisfying crunch and a refreshing flavor, making them an ideal snack for those looking for a light, protein-packed option. This dish combines the lean protein of boiled chicken breast with the crisp texture of celery, seasoned with a salt-free spice blend for added taste without the extra sodium.

**Ingredients for 1 serving:**
- 1/2 cup boiled chicken breast, chopped
- 1/2 cup celery, chopped
- 1 teaspoon salt-free spice blend (such as Italian seasoning or lemon pepper)
- Salt and pepper, to taste

**Preparation time**: 10 minutes
**Cooking time**: 15 minutes (for boiling chicken)

**Directions:**
1. Boil the Chicken: In a medium pot, bring water to a boil. Add the chicken breast and cook for about 15 minutes or until fully cooked. Remove from water and let cool.
2. Chop the Ingredients: Once cooled, chop the chicken breast into bite-sized pieces. Chop the celery into small pieces.
3. Mix and Season: In a bowl, combine the chopped chicken and celery. Sprinkle with the salt-free spice blend, and season with salt and pepper to taste.
4. Serve: Serve immediately as a snack or refrigerate for later.

**Nutritional value per serving:**
- Calories: 80- Carbs: 2g- Fiber: 1g- Sugars: 1g- Protein: 14g- Saturated Fat: 0g- Unsaturated Fat: 0g

**Difficulty rating**: ★☆☆☆☆

## 80. Melon Balls and Mint

**Introduction**:
Melon Balls and Mint is a refreshing and hydrating snack that combines the sweet juiciness of watermelon and cantaloupe with the cool, aromatic notes of fresh mint. This simple yet elegant dish is perfect for hot days or as a light snack to cleanse the palate.

**Ingredients for 1 serving:**
- 1/2 cup watermelon, balled
- 1/2 cup cantaloupe, balled
- 1 tablespoon fresh mint, finely chopped

**Preparation time**: 10 minutes
**Cooking time**: None

**Directions**:
1. Prepare the Melon Balls: Using a melon baller, scoop out balls from the watermelon and cantaloupe.
2. Combine and Add Mint: Place the melon balls in a serving bowl. Sprinkle with freshly chopped mint.
3. Serve: Serve immediately as a refreshing snack.

**Nutritional value per serving:**
- Calories: 50- Carbs: 13g- Fiber: 1g- Sugars: 11g- Protein: 1g- Saturated Fat: 0g- Unsaturated Fat: 0g

**Difficulty rating**: ★☆☆☆☆

# 81. Apple Slices and Cinnamon

**Introduction:**
Apple Slices and Cinnamon is a simple yet delightful snack that combines the crisp sweetness of apples with the warm, aromatic flavor of cinnamon. This classic combination is perfect for a quick and healthy snack, offering both a satisfying crunch and a hint of natural sweetness.

**Ingredients for 1 serving:**
- 1 medium apple, thinly sliced
- 1/4 teaspoon ground cinnamon

**Preparation time**: 5 minutes
**Cooking time**: None

**Directions:**
1. Prepare the Apple: Wash and thinly slice the apple, removing the core.
2. Add Cinnamon: Arrange the apple slices on a plate and sprinkle evenly with ground cinnamon.
3. Serve: Enjoy immediately as a refreshing and naturally sweet snack.

**Nutritional value per serving:**
- Calories: 80- Carbs: 22g- Fiber: 4g- Sugars: 16g- Protein: 0g- Saturated Fat: 0g- Unsaturated Fat: 0g

**Difficulty rating**: ★☆☆☆☆

# 82. Berry Yogurt Parfait

**Introduction:**
Berry Yogurt Parfait is a visually appealing and nutrient-packed snack that layers the tartness of plain nonfat yogurt with the sweetness of mixed berries. This parfait is not only delicious but also rich in antioxidants and protein, making it a perfect choice for a health-conscious snack or light breakfast.

**Ingredients for 1 serving:**
- 1/2 cup plain nonfat Greek yogurt
- 1/2 cup mixed berries (strawberries, blueberries, raspberries)
- 1 teaspoon honey (optional, if not strict on 0 points)

**Preparation time**: 5 minutes
**Cooking time**: None

**Directions**:
1. Prepare the Ingredients: Wash the berries and set them aside.
2. Layer the Parfait: In a glass, layer half of the yogurt, followed by a layer of mixed berries. Add another layer of yogurt and top with the remaining berries.
3. Optional Sweetener: Drizzle with honey if desired.
4. Serve: Serve immediately and enjoy the refreshing layers of flavor and texture.

**Nutritional value per serving:**
- Calories: 120 (without honey)- Carbs: 18g- Fiber: 4g- Sugars: 14g- Protein: 10g- Saturated Fat: 0g- Unsaturated Fat: 0g

**Difficulty rating**: ★☆☆☆☆

## 8.2 *Simple Side Dishes*

# 83. Steamed Asparagus

**Introduction:**
Steamed Asparagus is a classic and elegant side dish, perfect for pairing with a variety of main courses. The natural flavors of the asparagus are enhanced with a touch of lemon zest and a sprinkle of pepper, making it a refreshing and nutritious addition to any meal.

**Ingredients for 1 serving:**
- 8 asparagus spears, trimmed
- 1 teaspoon lemon zest
- Freshly ground black pepper to taste

**Preparation time**: 5 minutes

**Cooking time**: 5 minutes

**Directions:**
1. Prepare the Asparagus: Wash and trim the asparagus spears, cutting off the woody ends.
2. Steam the Asparagus: Place the asparagus in a steamer basket over boiling water. Cover and steam for 5 minutes or until tender-crisp.
3. Season and Serve: Transfer the asparagus to a serving plate. Sprinkle with lemon zest and freshly ground black pepper. Serve immediately.

**Nutritional value per serving:**
- Calories: 20- Carbs: 4g- Fiber: 2g- Sugars: 2g- Protein: 2g- Saturated Fat: 0g- Unsaturated Fat: 0g

**Difficulty rating**: ★☆☆☆☆

# 84. Garlic Cauliflower Mash

**Introduction:**
Garlic Cauliflower Mash is a delicious and healthier alternative to traditional mashed potatoes. This dish features steamed cauliflower mashed to a creamy consistency, flavored with garlic, and seasoned with a touch of salt, offering a satisfying side dish that's both low in calories and carbs.

**Ingredients for 1 serving:**
- 1/2 medium head of cauliflower, cut into florets
- 1 clove garlic, minced
- A pinch of salt
- Freshly ground black pepper to taste

**Preparation time**: 10 minutes
**Cooking time**: 10 minutes

**Directions:**
1. Steam the Cauliflower: Place cauliflower florets in a steamer basket over boiling water. Cover and steam for 8-10 minutes or until the cauliflower is tender.
2. Mash the Cauliflower: Transfer the steamed cauliflower to a bowl. Add minced garlic and a pinch of salt. Use a potato masher or blender to mash the cauliflower until smooth.
3. Season and Serve: Season the mash with freshly ground black pepper to taste. Serve hot as a side dish.

**Nutritional value per serving:**
- Calories: 30- Carbs: 5g- Fiber: 2g- Sugars: 2g- Protein: 2g- Saturated Fat: 0g- Unsaturated Fat: 0g

**Difficulty rating**: ★☆☆☆☆

# 85. Carrot and Ginger Soup

**Introduction:**
Carrot and Ginger Soup is a warm and comforting side dish, perfect for any season. The natural sweetness of carrots is beautifully complemented by the spiciness of ginger, creating a rich and flavorful soup that's both nourishing and satisfying.

**Ingredients for 1 serving:**
- 2 large carrots, peeled and chopped
- 1-inch piece of ginger, peeled and grated
- 1 cup vegetable broth (low sodium)
- Salt and pepper to taste

**Preparation time**: 10 minutes
**Cooking time**: 20 minutes

**Directions:**
1. Prepare the Vegetables: Peel and chop the carrots into small pieces. Peel and grate the ginger.
2. Cook the Soup: In a medium saucepan, combine the carrots, ginger, and vegetable broth. Bring to a boil, then reduce the heat and simmer for about 20 minutes, or until the carrots are tender.
3. Blend and Season: Using an immersion blender or regular blender, puree the soup until smooth. Season with salt and pepper to taste.
4. Serve: Ladle the soup into bowls and serve warm.

**Nutritional value per serving:**
- Calories: 80- Carbs: 19g- Fiber: 4g- Sugars: 10g- Protein: 2g- Saturated Fat: 0g- Unsaturated Fat: 0g

**Difficulty rating**: ★☆☆☆☆

# 86. Sautéed Spinach with Garlic

**Introduction:**
Sautéed Spinach with Garlic is a quick and nutritious side dish that pairs well with a variety of main courses. The garlic adds a delicious aroma and flavor, while the spinach provides essential nutrients, making it a healthy addition to your meal.

**Ingredients for 1 serving:**
- 2 cups fresh spinach leaves
- 1 clove garlic, minced

- 1 teaspoon olive oil (optional, adjust points if using)
- Salt and pepper to taste
- A splash of lemon juice

**Preparation time**: 5 minutes
**Cooking time**: 5 minutes

**Directions:**
1. Prepare the Ingredients: Rinse the spinach leaves thoroughly. Mince the garlic.
2. Sauté the Garlic: In a large skillet, heat the olive oil over medium heat (if using). Add the minced garlic and sauté for 1-2 minutes until fragrant.
3. Cook the Spinach: Add the spinach to the skillet and cook, stirring occasionally, until wilted, about 2-3 minutes.
4. Season and Serve: Season with salt, pepper, and a splash of lemon juice. Serve immediately.

**Nutritional value per serving:**
- Calories: 40 (without olive oil)- Carbs: 6g- Fiber: 2g- Sugars: 0g- Protein: 2g- Saturated Fat: 0g- Unsaturated Fat: 0g

**Difficulty rating**: ★☆☆☆☆

## 87. Mixed Greens Salad

**Introduction:**
This Mixed Greens Salad is a fresh and vibrant addition to any meal, offering a delightful blend of textures and flavors. The crispness of arugula and romaine lettuce, combined with a light lemon juice dressing, makes this a refreshing and healthy side dish.

**Ingredients for 1 serving:**
- 2 cups mixed greens (arugula, romaine, and other leafy greens)
- Juice of 1/2 lemon
- Salt and pepper to taste

**Preparation time**: 5 minutes
**Cooking time**: None

**Directions:**
1. Prepare the Greens: Rinse and dry the mixed greens thoroughly.
2. Dress the Salad: In a large bowl, toss the greens with lemon juice. Season with salt and pepper to taste.
3. Serve: Plate the salad and enjoy it as a light and refreshing side.

**Nutritional value per serving:**
- Calories: 20- Carbs: 4g- Fiber: 2g- Sugars: 1g- Protein: 1g- Saturated Fat: 0g- Unsaturated Fat: 0g

**Difficulty rating**: ★☆☆☆☆

## 88. Balsamic Roasted Tomatoes

**Introduction:**
Balsamic Roasted Tomatoes are a simple yet flavorful side dish that brings out the natural sweetness of cherry tomatoes. Roasting them with balsamic vinegar and fresh basil adds a rich, tangy flavor, perfect for pairing with a variety of main dishes.

**Ingredients for 1 serving:**
- 1 cup cherry tomatoes, halved
- 1 tablespoon balsamic vinegar
- Fresh basil leaves, torn
- Salt and pepper to taste

**Preparation time**: 5 minutes
**Cooking time**: 20 minutes

**Directions:**
1. Preheat the Oven: Preheat your oven to 375°F (190°C).
2. Prepare the Tomatoes: Place the halved cherry tomatoes in a baking dish. Drizzle with balsamic vinegar, and season with salt and pepper. Toss to coat evenly.
3. Roast the Tomatoes: Roast in the preheated oven for about 20 minutes, or until the tomatoes are soft and slightly caramelized.
4. Add Basil and Serve: Remove from the oven, sprinkle with fresh basil leaves, and serve warm.

**Nutritional value per serving:**
- Calories: 40- Carbs: 7g- Fiber: 2g- Sugars: 5g- Protein: 1g- Saturated Fat: 0g- Unsaturated Fat: 0g

**Difficulty rating**: ★☆☆☆☆

## 89. Zucchini Noodles

**Introduction:**
Zucchini Noodles, often referred to as "zoodles," are a light and nutritious alternative to traditional pasta. This dish highlights the fresh, delicate flavor of zucchini, complemented by a simple garlic sauté, making it a perfect side dish or base for other toppings.

**Ingredients for 1 serving:**
- 1 medium zucchini, spiralized
- 1 clove garlic, minced
- 1 teaspoon olive oil (optional, use cooking spray for 0 points)
- Salt and pepper to taste

**Preparation time**: 5 minutes
**Cooking time**: 5 minutes

**Directions:**
1. Spiralize the Zucchini: Using a spiralizer, create noodles from the zucchini. Set aside.
2. Sauté the Garlic: In a skillet, heat the olive oil (or cooking spray) over medium heat. Add the minced garlic and sauté until fragrant, about 1 minute.
3. Cook the Zoodles: Add the zucchini noodles to the skillet. Sauté for 2-3 minutes, or until just tender. Season with salt and pepper to taste.

4. Serve: Transfer to a plate and serve immediately, either as a side dish or topped with your choice of protein.

**Nutritional value per serving:**
- Calories: 40- Carbs: 7g- Fiber: 2g- Sugars: 4g- Protein: 2g- Saturated Fat: 0g- Unsaturated Fat: 0g

**Difficulty rating:** ★☆☆☆☆

# 90. Spicy Green Beans

**Introduction:**
Spicy Green Beans are a vibrant and flavorful side dish that combines the crisp texture of green beans with the heat of chili flakes. This quick and easy recipe is perfect for adding a spicy kick to your meal.

**Ingredients for 1 serving:**
- 1 cup green beans, trimmed
- 1 clove garlic, minced
- 1/4 teaspoon chili flakes (adjust to taste)
- 1 teaspoon olive oil (optional, use cooking spray for 0 points)
- Salt to taste

**Preparation time:** 5 minutes
**Cooking time:** 7 minutes

**Directions:**
1. Prepare the Green Beans: Rinse and trim the green beans. Set aside.
2. Heat the Skillet: In a large skillet, heat the olive oil (or cooking spray) over medium heat. Add the minced garlic and chili flakes, and sauté for 1 minute, being careful not to burn the garlic.
3. Sauté the Green Beans: Add the green beans to the skillet. Sauté for 5-6 minutes, or until they are tender-crisp. Season with salt to taste.
4. Serve: Transfer the spicy green beans to a serving dish and enjoy hot.

**Nutritional value per serving:**
- Calories: 50- Carbs: 10g- Fiber: 4g- Sugars: 4g- Protein: 2g- Saturated Fat: 0g- Unsaturated Fat: 0g

**Difficulty rating:** ★☆☆☆☆

# 91. Roasted Bell Peppers

**Introduction:**
Roasted Bell Peppers are a versatile and colorful addition to any meal. Their natural sweetness is enhanced through roasting, and they can be enjoyed warm or chilled, making them an excellent side dish for any occasion.

**Ingredients for 1 serving:**
- 2 large bell peppers (any color)
- 1 teaspoon olive oil (optional, use cooking spray for 0 points)
- 1 teaspoon mixed herbs (such as thyme, rosemary, or oregano)
- Salt and pepper to taste

**Preparation time**: 10 minutes
**Cooking time**: 25 minutes

**Directions:**
1. Preheat the Oven: Preheat your oven to 400°F (200°C).
2. Prepare the Peppers: Wash and dry the bell peppers. Cut them into halves or quarters, removing the seeds and membranes.
3. Season the Peppers: Place the bell pepper pieces on a baking sheet lined with parchment paper. Drizzle with olive oil or lightly spray with cooking spray. Sprinkle with mixed herbs, salt, and pepper.
4. Roast the Peppers: Roast in the preheated oven for 20-25 minutes, or until the peppers are tender and slightly charred around the edges.
5. Serve: Remove from the oven and let cool slightly before serving. These peppers can be enjoyed warm or at room temperature.

**Nutritional value per serving:**
- Calories: 80- Carbs: 18g- Fiber: 4g- Sugars: 12g- Protein: 2g- Saturated Fat: 0g- Unsaturated Fat: 0g

**Difficulty rating**: ★☆☆☆☆

## *8.3 DIPS AND DRESSINGS*

# 92. Salsa Verde

**Introduction**:
Salsa Verde is a zesty and refreshing dip, perfect for pairing with raw vegetables, lean proteins, or even as a topping for grilled dishes. This vibrant green sauce is full of fresh flavors and a bit of a spicy kick.

**Ingredients for 1 serving**:
- 3 tomatillos, husked and rinsed
- 1/4 cup fresh cilantro leaves
- 1 jalapeño, seeded and chopped (adjust to taste)
- Juice of 1 lime
- 1/4 teaspoon salt
- 1 clove garlic

**Preparation time**: 10 minutes
**Cooking time**: None

**Directions:**
1. Prepare the Ingredients: Roughly chop the tomatillos and jalapeño.
2. Blend: Combine all ingredients in a blender or food processor.
3. Blend Until Smooth: Process until the mixture is smooth and well combined.
4. Taste and Adjust: Taste the salsa and adjust the seasoning with more lime juice or salt if necessary.
5. Serve: Serve immediately or refrigerate for up to 3 days.

**Nutritional value per serving:**
- Calories: 25- Carbs: 5g- Fiber: 2g- Sugars: 3g- Protein: 1g- Saturated Fat: 0g- Unsaturated Fat: 0g

**Difficulty rating**: ★☆☆☆☆

# 93. Herb Yogurt Dip

**Introduction**:
This creamy and refreshing dip is made from plain nonfat Greek yogurt and a medley of fresh herbs. It's perfect for dipping vegetables, spreading on wraps, or even as a salad dressing.

**Ingredients for 1 serving:**
- 1/2 cup plain nonfat Greek yogurt
- 1 tablespoon fresh dill, chopped
- 1 tablespoon fresh parsley, chopped
- 1 clove garlic, minced
- Juice of 1/2 lemon
- Salt and pepper to taste

**Preparation time**: 5 minutes
**Cooking time**: None

**Directions**:
1. Combine Ingredients: In a small bowl, mix together the Greek yogurt, dill, parsley, and garlic.
2. Season: Add lemon juice, salt, and pepper to taste.
3. Stir: Stir until all ingredients are well incorporated.
4. Serve: Serve immediately or chill for an hour to let the flavors meld.

**Nutritional value per serving**:
- Calories: 60- Carbs: 6g- Fiber: 0g- Sugars: 4g- Protein: 10g- Saturated Fat: 0g- Unsaturated Fat: 0g

**Difficulty rating**: ★☆☆☆☆

## 94. Spicy Tomato Salsa

**Introduction**:
This Spicy Tomato Salsa is a classic accompaniment for a variety of dishes. It's bursting with fresh flavors from ripe tomatoes, onions, cilantro, and a kick of jalapeño, making it a versatile and healthy addition to your meals.

**Ingredients for 1 serving:**
- 2 ripe tomatoes, diced
- 1/4 cup red onion, finely chopped
- 1 jalapeño, seeded and finely chopped
- 1/4 cup fresh cilantro, chopped
- Juice of 1 lime
- Salt to taste

**Preparation time**: 10 minutes
**Cooking time**: None

**Directions:**
1. Prepare Ingredients: Dice the tomatoes and chop the onion, jalapeño, and cilantro.
2. Mix: In a bowl, combine all the ingredients.
3. Season: Add lime juice and salt, adjusting to taste.
4. Serve: Stir well and serve immediately or refrigerate for up to 2 days.

**Nutritional value per serving:**
- Calories: 25- Carbs: 6g- Fiber: 2g- Sugars: 4g- Protein: 1g- Saturated Fat: 0g- Unsaturated Fat: 0g

**Difficulty rating:** ★☆☆☆☆

## 95. Cucumber Dill Dressing

**Introduction**:
This light and refreshing dressing combines the coolness of cucumber with the aromatic flavor of dill, creating a perfect accompaniment for salads or as a dip for fresh vegetables.

**Ingredients for 1 serving:**
- 1/2 cup plain nonfat Greek yogurt
- 1/2 cucumber, peeled and diced
- 1 tablespoon fresh dill, chopped
- 1 clove garlic, minced

- Juice of 1/2 lemon
- Salt and pepper to taste

**Preparation time**: 5 minutes
**Cooking time**: None

**Directions:**
1. Prepare Ingredients: Dice the cucumber and chop the dill.
2. Blend: In a blender, combine all the ingredients until smooth.
3. Season: Taste and adjust seasoning with salt and pepper as needed.
4. Serve: Chill in the refrigerator for at least 30 minutes before serving to allow the flavors to meld.

**Nutritional value per serving:**
- Calories: 60- Carbs: 6g- Fiber: 0g- Sugars: 4g- Protein: 10g- Saturated Fat: 0g- Unsaturated Fat: 0g

**Difficulty rating**: ★☆☆☆☆

## 96. Garlic and Lemon Dressing

**Introduction:**
This vibrant dressing is a simple yet flavorful blend of garlic and lemon juice, enhanced with a hint of mustard. It's perfect for brightening up any salad or as a zesty marinade for grilled vegetables.

**Ingredients for 1 serving:**
- 2 cloves garlic, minced
- Juice of 1 lemon
- 1 teaspoon Dijon mustard
- 1/4 teaspoon salt
- 1/4 teaspoon black pepper

**Preparation time**: 5 minutes
**Cooking time**: None

**Directions:**
1. Combine Ingredients: In a small bowl, whisk together garlic, lemon juice, and mustard.
2. Season: Add salt and pepper to taste.
3. Stir: Stir well to combine.
4. Serve: Use immediately or store in an airtight container in the refrigerator for up to one week.

**Nutritional value per serving**:
- Calories: 10- Carbs: 2g- Fiber: 0g- Sugars: 1g- Protein: 0g- Saturated Fat: 0g- Unsaturated Fat: 0g

**Difficulty rating**: ★☆☆☆☆

## 97. Apple Cider Vinegar Dressing

**Introduction**:
This tangy and slightly sweet dressing is made with apple cider vinegar and a touch of zero-point sweetener, perfect for adding a burst of flavor to your salads without extra calories.

**Ingredients for 1 serving**:
- 2 tablespoons apple cider vinegar
- 1 teaspoon Dijon mustard
- 1 teaspoon zero-point sweetener (like Stevia or Splenda)
- 1/4 teaspoon salt
- 1/4 teaspoon black pepper

**Preparation time**: 5 minutes
**Cooking time**: None

**Directions**:
1. Mix Ingredients: In a small bowl, whisk together apple cider vinegar, mustard, and sweetener.
2. Season: Add salt and pepper to taste.
3. Blend: Mix until fully combined and smooth.
4. Serve: Use immediately or refrigerate in a sealed container for up to one week.

**Nutritional value per serving**:
- Calories: 5- Carbs: 1g- Fiber: 0g- Sugars: 0g- Protein: 0g- Saturated Fat: 0g- Unsaturated Fat: 0g

**Difficulty rating**: ★☆☆☆☆

## 98. Mint Chutney

**Introduction:**
This refreshing mint chutney offers a zesty kick, perfect for adding vibrant flavor to grilled meats, salads, or as a dip for fresh vegetables. The combination of fresh mint, cilantro, and lime juice creates a bright, tangy sauce with a hint of spice from green chili.

**Ingredients for 1 serving:**
- 1 cup fresh mint leaves
- 1/2 cup fresh cilantro leaves
- Juice of 1 lime
- 1 small green chili, chopped (seeds removed for less heat)
- 1 clove garlic, minced
- Salt to taste

**Preparation time**: 5 minutes
**Cooking time**: None

**Directions:**
1. Prepare Ingredients: Wash the mint and cilantro leaves thoroughly and pat them dry.
2. Blend: In a blender or food processor, combine the mint, cilantro, lime juice, green chili, and garlic.
3. Season: Add salt to taste.
4. Blend Until Smooth: Pulse until the mixture is smooth, scraping down the sides as needed.
5. Serve: Use immediately or store in an airtight container in the refrigerator for up to three days.

**Nutritional value per serving:**
- Calories: 15- Carbs: 3g- Fiber: 1g- Sugars: 0g- Protein: 0g- Saturated Fat: 0g- Unsaturated Fat: 0g

**Difficulty rating**: ★☆☆☆☆

# 99. Zesty Lime Salsa

**Introduction:**
This zesty lime salsa is a fresh and tangy addition to any meal. It pairs well with grilled chicken or fish, or as a refreshing topping for salads. The combination of tomatoes, onions, lime zest, and cilantro creates a vibrant, flavorful dip.

**Ingredients for 1 serving:**
- 2 medium tomatoes, chopped
- 1/2 small red onion, finely chopped
- Zest of 1 lime
- Juice of 1 lime
- 1/4 cup fresh cilantro, chopped
- Salt and pepper to taste

**Preparation time**: 10 minutes
**Cooking time**: None

**Directions:**
1. Chop Ingredients: Finely chop the tomatoes and red onion.
2. Combine Ingredients: In a mixing bowl, combine the tomatoes, onion, lime zest, lime juice, and cilantro.
3. Season: Add salt and pepper to taste.
4. Mix Well: Stir the ingredients together until well combined.
5. Serve: Enjoy immediately or refrigerate for up to two days to allow the flavors to meld.

**Nutritional value per serving:**
- Calories: 20- Carbs: 5g- Fiber: 1g- Sugars: 3g- Protein: 1g- Saturated Fat: 0g- Unsaturated Fat: 0g

**Difficulty rating**: ★☆☆☆☆

# CHAPTER 9

# OVERCOMING DIETARY CHALLENGES

## 9.1 How to Handle Eating Out

Navigating dining out while adhering to a specific dietary plan can be daunting. The array of tempting options, the ambiance, and the company all contribute to an environment where it's easy to stray from one's nutritional goals. However, with careful planning and mindful choices, eating out can still be an enjoyable and guilt-free experience. The key lies in preparation, strategic menu choices, and effective communication with restaurant staff.

**Preparation is Key**: Before heading to a restaurant, take a few moments to review the menu online. Most eateries provide their menus on their websites, and some even include nutritional information. Familiarize yourself with dishes that align with your dietary goals. Identify those that are grilled, steamed, baked, or raw, as these preparation methods are generally healthier compared to fried or breaded options.

**Strategic Menu Choices**: When perusing the menu, look for keywords like "grilled," "steamed," "baked," "broiled," or "fresh," which often indicate healthier options. Salads can be a good choice, but be cautious of dressings and toppings that can add unnecessary calories. Opt for a simple vinegar or lemon dressing and ask for it on the side. Additionally, consider appetizers or side dishes as main meals, as they are often lighter. Portion control is also crucial; you can request a half-portion or share with a dining companion.

**Communication with Restaurant Staff**: Do not hesitate to communicate your dietary needs to the server. Politely ask for modifications, such as having sauces served on the side, substituting vegetables for fries, or excluding certain ingredients. Most restaurants are accommodating and willing to make adjustments. Furthermore, inquire about how dishes are prepared; for instance, ask if vegetables are cooked in butter or if meats are marinated in sugar-laden sauces. Being upfront can help you stay on track with your dietary goals while still enjoying a night out.

## 9.2 Managing Social Events and Gatherings

Social events and gatherings often revolve around food, making it challenging to adhere to a dietary plan. From family celebrations to workplace parties, these occasions can present an array of tempting foods and social pressures to indulge. However, with a proactive approach and some strategic planning, you can navigate these events while maintaining your dietary goals.

**Plan Ahead**: Before attending a social event, eat a small, satisfying meal or snack that aligns with your dietary plan. This can help curb hunger and reduce the temptation to overeat. If the event is a potluck, consider bringing a dish that you know is diet-friendly, ensuring there will be at least one option that suits your needs.

**Mindful Eating**: At the event, be mindful of portion sizes and try to fill your plate with healthier options first, such as vegetables, lean proteins, and fruits. Avoid lingering near the food table, as this can lead to mindless snacking. Engage in conversations away from the food area to keep your focus on the social aspect rather than the food.

**Handling Social Pressure**: It can be difficult to refuse food offers or explain dietary choices in a social setting. Politely declining food or drink with a simple, "No, thank you," is usually sufficient. If you feel comfortable, you can explain that you are following a specific dietary plan for health reasons. Most people will respect your decision. Remember, it's okay to be assertive about your dietary needs and preferences.

## *9.3 Coping with Cravings*

Cravings are a natural part of the human experience and can pose a significant challenge when trying to maintain a specific dietary plan. Understanding the root causes of cravings and developing strategies to manage them can help maintain dietary goals and prevent unplanned indulgences.

**Understanding Cravings**: Cravings can be triggered by a variety of factors, including emotional states, physical hunger, hormonal fluctuations, or simply the sight and smell of certain foods. Recognizing the triggers that lead to cravings is the first step in managing them. For instance, stress, boredom, or habit can all contribute to a desire for certain foods, particularly those high in sugar or fat.

**Healthy Alternatives**: When cravings strike, try to satisfy them with healthier alternatives. For example, if you crave something sweet, opt for fresh fruit or a small serving of yogurt with berries. If the craving is for something crunchy, consider raw vegetables with a flavorful dip. Keeping healthy snacks readily available can make it easier to resist less healthy options.

**Mindfulness and Distraction**: Sometimes cravings are a result of habit rather than true hunger. Engaging in a distracting activity, such as a walk, reading, or a hobby, can help shift focus away from the craving. Additionally, practicing mindfulness techniques, such as deep breathing or meditation, can help manage stress and reduce the intensity of cravings.

**Allowing Occasional Indulgences**: It's important to recognize that occasional indulgences are a normal part of life and can be included in a healthy diet without derailing overall progress. Planning for occasional treats can prevent feelings of deprivation, which can lead to binge eating. The key is moderation and balance, ensuring that indulgences are occasional and not a regular occurrence.

# CHAPTER 10

# 30-DAY CUSTOM MEAL PLAN

## Week 1

### DAY 1

- **Breakfast**: Hard-Boiled Eggs with Grape Tomatoes and Cucumber Slices
- **Lunch:** Cucumber and Dill Sticks
- **Dinner**: Salsa Verde
- **Snack**: Grilled Zucchini Slices

### DAY 2

- **Breakfast**: Apple Slices with Cinnamon
- **Lunch**: Grilled Zucchini Slices
- **Dinner**: Herb Yogurt Dip
- **Snack**: Fruit Salad

### DAY 3

- **Breakfast**: Protein-Packed Smoothie
- **Lunch**: Fruit Salad
- **Dinner**: Spicy Tomato Salsa
- **Snack**: Pickled Vegetables

### DAY 4

- **Breakfast**: Banana Pancakes
- **Lunch**: Pickled Vegetables
- **Dinner**: Cucumber Dill Dressing
- **Snack**: Chicken and Celery Bites

### DAY 5

- **Breakfast**: Fruit Kebabs
- **Lunch**: Chicken and Celery Bites
- **Dinner**: Garlic and Lemon Dressing
- **Snack**: Melon Balls and Mint

### DAY 6

- **Breakfast**: Veggie Capsicum Cups
- **Lunch**: Melon Balls and Mint
- **Dinner**: Apple Cider Vinegar Dressing
- **Snack**: Apple Slices and Cinnamon

### Day 7

- **Breakfast**: Cold Turkey Roll-Ups
- **Lunch**: Apple Slices and Cinnamon
- **Dinner**: Mint Chutney
- **Snack**: Berry Yogurt Parfait

## Week 2

### Day 8

- **Breakfast**: Mixed Berry Bowl
- **Lunch**: Berry Yogurt Parfait
- **Dinner**: Zesty Lime Salsa
- **Snack**: Steamed Asparagus

### Day 9

- **Breakfast**: Spicy Tomato Shakshuka
- **Lunch**: Steamed Asparagus
- **Dinner**: Salsa Verde
- **Snack**: Garlic Cauliflower Mash

### Day 10

- **Breakfast**: Turkey and Spinach Omelette
- **Lunch**: Garlic Cauliflower Mash
- **Dinner**: Herb Yogurt Dip
- **Snack**: Carrot and Ginger Soup

### Day 11

- **Breakfast**: Smoked Salmon and Cucumber Rolls
- **Lunch**: Carrot and Ginger Soup
- **Dinner**: Spicy Tomato Salsa
- **Snack**: Sautéed Spinach with Garlic

### Day 12

- **Breakfast**: Fruit Smoothie
- **Lunch**: Sautéed Spinach with Garlic
- **Dinner**: Cucumber Dill Dressing
- **Snack**: Mixed Greens Salad

### Day 13

- **Breakfast**: Egg White Scramble
- **Lunch**: Mixed Greens Salad
- **Dinner**: Garlic and Lemon Dressing
- **Snack**: Balsamic Roasted Tomatoes

### Day 14

- **Breakfast**: Grilled Chicken Salad
- **Lunch**: Balsamic Roasted Tomatoes
- **Dinner**: Apple Cider Vinegar Dressing
- **Snack**: Zucchini Noodles

## Week 3

### Day 15

- **Breakfast**: Vegetable Stir-Fry
- **Lunch**: Zucchini Noodles
- **Dinner**: Mint Chutney
- **Snack**: Spicy Green Beans

### Day 16

- **Breakfast**: Salsa Egg Muffins
- **Lunch**: Spicy Green Beans
- **Dinner**: Salsa Verde
- **Snack**: Roasted Bell Peppers

### Day 17

- **Breakfast**: Tofu and Veggie Scramble
- **Lunch**: Roasted Bell Peppers
- **Dinner**: Herb Yogurt Dip
- **Snack**: Cucumber and Dill Sticks

### Day 18

- **Breakfast**: Egg and Spinach Casserole
- **Lunch**: Cucumber and Dill Sticks
- **Dinner**: Spicy Tomato Salsa
- **Snack**: Grilled Zucchini Slices

### Day 19

- **Breakfast**: Zucchini and Egg Frittata
- **Lunch**: Grilled Zucchini Slices
- **Dinner**: Cucumber Dill Dressing
- **Snack**: Fruit Salad

### Day 20

- **Breakfast**: Cantaloupe and Berry Salad
- **Lunch**: Fruit Salad
- **Dinner**: Garlic and Lemon Dressing
- **Snack**: Pickled Vegetables

### Day 21

- **Breakfast**: Seafood Salad
- **Lunch**: Pickled Vegetables
- **Dinner**: Apple Cider Vinegar Dressing
- **Snack**: Chicken and Celery Bites

## Week 4

### Day 22

- **Breakfast**: Poached Eggs over Asparagus
- **Lunch**: Chicken and Celery Bites
- **Dinner**: Mint Chutney
- **Snack**: Melon Balls and Mint

### Day 23

- **Breakfast**: Mixed Vegetable Soup
- **Lunch**: Melon Balls and Mint
- **Dinner**: Zesty Lime Salsa
- **Snack**: Apple Slices and Cinnamon

### Day 24

- **Breakfast**: Herbed Chicken Skewers
- **Lunch**: Apple Slices and Cinnamon
- **Dinner**: Salsa Verde
- **Snack**: Berry Yogurt Parfait

### Day 25

- **Breakfast**: Cucumber and Yogurt Soup
- **Lunch**: Berry Yogurt Parfait
- **Dinner**: Herb Yogurt Dip
- **Snack**: Steamed Asparagus

### Day 26

- **Breakfast**: Greek Yogurt with Fresh Fruit
- **Lunch**: Steamed Asparagus
- **Dinner**: Spicy Tomato Salsa
- **Snack**: Garlic Cauliflower Mash

### Day 27

- **Breakfast**: Hard-Boiled Eggs with Grape Tomatoes and Cucumber Slices
- **Lunch**: Garlic Cauliflower Mash
- **Dinner**: Cucumber Dill Dressing
- **Snack**: Carrot and Ginger Soup

## Day 28

- **Breakfast**: Apple Slices with Cinnamon
- **Lunch**: Carrot and Ginger Soup
- **Dinner**: Garlic and Lemon Dressing
- **Snack**: Sautéed Spinach with Garlic

## Day 29

- **Breakfast**: Protein-Packed Smoothie
- **Lunch**: Sautéed Spinach with Garlic
- **Dinner**: Apple Cider Vinegar Dressing
- **Snack**: Mixed Greens Salad

## Day 30

- **Breakfast**: Banana Pancakes
- **Lunch**: Mixed Greens Salad
- **Dinner**: Mint Chutney
- **Snack**: Balsamic Roasted Tomatoes

# YOUR FREE GIFTS!

CLICK HERE TO DOWNLOAD

**SCAN HERE TO DOWNLOAD**

# CONCLUSION

**Embracing a Lifelong Healthy Eating Habit**

In the journey towards healthier living, the adoption of a nutritious eating pattern is not merely a short-term goal but a lifelong commitment. Embracing healthy eating habits involves more than just following a set diet plan; it's about developing a sustainable relationship with food. This journey requires an understanding of how different foods nourish the body and influence overall well-being. It involves making informed choices that prioritize nutrient-dense foods, which provide essential vitamins, minerals, and other nutrients critical for maintaining health.

A crucial aspect of this lifestyle change is the recognition that it's not about perfection but about balance and consistency. Everyone experiences moments of indulgence or deviation from their dietary goals, and it's important to approach these instances with a forgiving attitude. The focus should remain on the long-term pattern of eating rather than occasional slip-ups. This perspective helps in building a resilient mindset that can navigate the challenges and temptations that inevitably arise.

Moreover, healthy eating should be viewed as a dynamic and evolving process. As life circumstances change—such as aging, changing health conditions, or lifestyle adjustments—so too should dietary habits. This flexibility ensures that one's eating patterns continue to support health and well-being throughout different stages of life. By fostering a positive and proactive approach to food, individuals can enjoy the pleasures of eating while maintaining a balanced diet that supports their health goals.

**How to Stay Inspired**

Maintaining motivation is a key challenge in any long-term lifestyle change, and healthy eating is no exception. Staying inspired requires regular reminders of why these changes are important and the benefits they bring. One effective strategy is to set clear, achievable goals and celebrate the progress made towards these milestones. Whether it's improved energy levels, better health markers, or simply feeling more confident, acknowledging these benefits can reinforce the desire to continue. Another powerful motivator is to keep the experience of eating enjoyable and engaging. This can be achieved by exploring new recipes, trying different cuisines, and continually learning about nutrition. Keeping meals varied and flavorful not only prevents monotony but also ensures a wide intake of nutrients. Involvement in cooking and meal preparation can also deepen one's appreciation for food, making healthy choices more appealing.

Connecting with others who share similar goals can provide valuable support and encouragement. Whether through online communities, local groups, or friends and family, sharing experiences and challenges can foster a sense of community and accountability. Engaging with a support network helps individuals stay focused and motivated, offering both practical advice and emotional encouragement. It's also helpful to remember that motivation fluctuates naturally. During low periods, revisiting initial motivations, such as improved health or setting a positive example for loved ones, can help rekindle enthusiasm. Visual reminders, such as a vision board or a journal, can also serve as daily inspiration to stay committed to healthy eating habits.

**Continuing Your Education in Health and Nutrition**

The landscape of nutrition and health is constantly evolving, with new research and insights emerging regularly. To maintain a lifelong commitment to healthy eating, it's essential to stay informed and educated about these developments. This ongoing education helps individuals make better dietary choices and adapt to new information as it becomes available.

One practical approach is to engage with credible sources of nutrition information, such as registered dietitians, reputable health organizations, and scientific journals. These sources provide reliable guidance that can help navigate the complexities of nutrition science. It's also valuable to develop critical thinking skills to discern between scientifically supported advice and popular diet myths or trends.

Continuing education can also involve exploring various aspects of nutrition beyond the basics. This might include understanding the nutritional needs at different life stages, the impact of food on specific health conditions, or the environmental and ethical considerations of food choices. Expanding knowledge in these areas can enrich one's understanding of health and wellness and inspire more thoughtful dietary choices.

Additionally, participating in workshops, cooking classes, or seminars can provide hands-on learning opportunities and expose individuals to new foods and cooking techniques. These experiences not only enhance culinary skills but also deepen the appreciation for the role of food in overall well-being.

Ultimately, staying curious and open-minded about nutrition fosters a proactive approach to health. By continually learning and adapting, individuals can sustain their commitment to healthy eating and enjoy the many benefits it brings throughout life.

# INDEX

## T



## V



## Z

Made in the USA
Columbia, SC
06 October 2024